EVALUATING SUSTAINABLE DEVELOPMENT

EVALUATING
SUSTAINABLE
DEVELOPMENT

Giving People a Voice
in Their Destiny

Okechukwu Ukaga and Chris Maser

STERLING, VIRGINIA

Published in 2004 by

Stylus Publishing, LLC
22883 Quicksilver Drive
Sterling, Virginia 20166

**Library of Congress
Cataloging-in-Publication Data**
Ukaga, Okechukwu, 1961–
    Evaluating sustainable development: giving
        people a voice in their destiny/
        Okechukwu Ukaga and Chris Maser—
        1st ed.
    ISBN 1-57922-0827 (alk. paper)—
    ISBN 1-57922-0835 (pbk. : alk. paper)
    1. Economic development projects—
    Evaluation. 2. Sustainable development—
    citizen participation.

HC79.44.U38 2004
338.9/27 22
2003016290

Our political leaders have failed us in three major areas: in challenge, in faithfulness, and in candor. . . . There is, however, a second half to the equation, for citizens—followers—owe their country something that they too have failed to give. All too often our people look for the easy answer and for leaders who, in the words of Sidney Harris, will "reconcile the irreconcilable . . . and promise us a society where we can continue to be as narrow and envious and shortsighted as we like without suffering the consequences." So as citizens we have some obligations to fulfill, too, and foremost among them is an honest assessment of where we are headed.

Morris K. Udall

CONTENTS

A strong organizing context perceived from many points of view, such as a shared community vision, establishes the need to evaluate the results of implementing the community's vision and determines what needs to be evaluated and how. For a community to become sustainable, it must be able to understand its life-support systems and how they influence and are influenced by a variety of factors, which makes evaluation imperative.

Although the term "evaluation" is variously used, it's meaning here is simply to assess, monitor, grade, or judge the intended outcomes and/or unintended effects of specific activities on a particular system. Evaluation, in this sense, includes a formal process of observing and interpreting the overall results of such human activities as urban development, logging, and farming in relation to the biophysical and social variables associated with those activities (for example, increases in air pollution with urban growth and increases in soil erosion with logging and farming).

Like a microscope or a telescope, evaluation acts as a lens through which we humans detect events and trends not normally within the range of our perception. For example, only long-term, global-scale evaluation can determine the consequences of the "greenhouse effect" on the Earth's atmosphere (first proposed as a theory in 1894 by a Swedish scientist studying the effects of burning fossil fuels), which in turn affects the quality of human life and perhaps even human survival. Here a caution from professor John Gray, of the London School of Economics, is advisable: "If we redesign nature to fit human wishes, we risk making it [Nature] a mirror of our limitations."

Evaluation of sustainable development emphasizes the process of decision making based on the analysis of perceived risk. Decision making is therefore steeped in questions surrounding risk: How much risk are we capable of handling? What magnitude of risk are we willing to assume by our collective action or inaction? What are the consequences of that risk? Can they even be measured? If so, how? If not, why not?

There are two basic approaches to dealing with uncertainty. First, as we have traditionally done, we can seek to increase our knowledge in order to decrease the uncertainty associated with manipulating ecosystems. Second, and still largely untried, we can act more cautiously. The latter approach assumes that, in our ignorance, the risks of making mistakes outweigh the potential payoff of being correct. A farmer decides to not grow a certain cash crop because she is unwilling to assume the risk of a potential increase in soil erosion that might subsequently cause a decline in her economic productivity.

As this example depicts, evaluation and subsequent decision making can be rather straightforward on a small farm. In such a place, disasters occur at the personal scale of an event between a farmer and Nature.

On the other hand, decision making is more impersonal and vastly more complex and tenuous in agribusiness, in a national forest, or within the reciprocal relationship of a community to its landscape. Such decisions are not only made in a collective but also laden with corporate and social values, especially within the immediate vicinity of a community working it's way toward sustainability. At this scale, evaluation closes the circle of knowledge with respect to outcomes at the interface between Nature and society, as opposed to Nature and the individual.

Social-environmental sustainability is only as vibrant and successful as the psychological maturity of those involved in the process. We say this because our experience has been that those people in a community who tend toward psychological maturity speak for the children (present and future), whereas those who tend toward psychological immaturity speak only for themselves. With the former, sustainability is possible. With the later, it is not—because the children have no voice.

According to American poet John Ashbery, "tomorrow is easy, but today is uncharted." "This observation," says professor John Gray, "points out our real human weakness, which is not our incurable ignorance of the future, but rather our failure to understand the present. And it is the present in terms of the future that evaluation addresses."

In this book, we present a basic philosophy and the tools for participatory evaluation of sustainable development. We acknowledge that concepts, challenges, opportunities, and circumstances surrounding sustainable development can differ significantly from one place or group to another.* It is precisely such variations that make it critical for all the "stakeholders" to play the dominant roles in planning and implementing their own evaluation. By stakeholders, we mean all those whose interest could be impacted in one way or the other by the proposed venture. Having all interested parties represented in the key evaluation roles is the best way to assure that the circumstances and values of the general populace are accounted for in terms of community sustainability.

The first chapter of the book gives a brief introduction to the concepts of sustainable development and the role evaluation plays. With this as a framework, the rest of the book covers: planning an evaluation; collecting the data; analyzing and interpreting the data; and using the findings. The book concludes with practical suggestions for planning and implementing an evaluation.

---

* Detailed discussion of such variations is beyond the scope of this book.

ACKNOWLEDGMENTS

We thank the following people (listed in alphabetical order) for their thoughtful review of our manuscript and suggestions for improving some parts: Emmanuel Enemouh, Bill Fleischman, Terry Gips, Dick Kruger, Mike Mageau, Ron Regal, and Nick Salafsky.

I also thank: Ed Yoder for nurturing my interest in evaluation and research methods; Maurice Albertson for encouraging me to write something on evaluation of sustainable development; and Susan Seabury for helping me type three of the figures in the book. And finally, I am very grateful to my wife, Chi, and children Okey Jr., Emeka, Gozie, and Ekeoma for their love, support, and understanding as I spent many hours after my regular work time, writing and revising the manuscript.—Okey

As always, I thank Zane, my lovely wife for her patience with me as I worked on this book.—Chris

I

SUSTAINABLE DEVELOPMENT AND EVALUATION

In its 1987 report, *Our Common Future*, the World Commission on Environment and Development defined sustainable development as "development that meets the needs of the present without compromising the ability of future generations to meet their own needs."[1] This definition attempts to address the complex relationship between the environment and development. Although the concept of sustainable development draws on two potentially opposed traditions, "development," which implies continual, physical growth, and "sustainable," which implies conservation or maintenance of the status quo, it means more than simply seeking a compromise between them.[2]

Although some people feel the notion of "sustainable development," is an oxymoron, it is not. Sustainable development addresses the total quality of life by meeting current human necessities while protecting the ability of future generations to meet their own. Such necessities include the environment's ability to provide resources, recycle waste, and maintain a rich biodiversity, genetic diversity, and functional diversity on a sustainable basis.

Some frameworks of sustainable development include the: Hanover Principle, Natural Step System Conditions, Herman Daly rules, Holistic Management Model, Bellagio Principles, and Earth Charter 2000, to name just a few. While each framework is somewhat different and reflects the perspectives of its authors, there are generally some common themes that run through all such frameworks:

- A long-term, holistic perspective
- Responsibility and accountability
- Systems thinking
- Paying attention to the ecological carrying capacity
- Meeting human necessities fairly and efficiently
- Preserving options for both present and future generations to their needs
- Community well-being based on broad participation
- Conservation and minimization of waste
- Cooperation and coordination
- Equality of race, gender, etc.
- Maintaining the diversity and productivity of nature
- Participatory decision making
- Prudence and precaution
- Shared responsibility
- Right of all citizens to empower themselves
- Linking various aspects of sustainability (that is, economic, ecological, and social)

A good understanding of the basic principles and concepts of sustainable development is essential for appropriately evaluating projects or phenomenon that deal with sustainable development itself. This understanding is important because the basis for evaluating sustainable development must both reflect and relate to the principles and philosophy of sustainability as the foundation of the evaluation process because these values must be accounted for. Therefore, any group planning to evaluate a given initiative or event must have a good conversation about their philosophy with respect to sustainability so they can develop the aims and purposes of the evaluation to be consistent with their stated values.

Where people stand on specific principles of sustainable development determines the questions they ask, how they interpret and use data, and the positions they take on specific issues. Further, the context and concepts of sustainable development may differ considerably from one group to the other and across various settings.

For instance, while all are interested in the long-term global objectives of sustainable development, the countries and communities that are yet to satisfactorily meet their basic human necessities, tend to be more interested in an agenda of sustainable development that seeks to "enhance their current and future potentials to meet human needs and aspirations."[3] As Professor Geoffrey Nwaka noted, there is a growing distinction between the agenda for long-term global environmental security and the agenda for environmental issues associated with the immediate problems of survival and development in non-industrialized countries.[4]

For citizens in these countries, the "ecological debt" owed to future generations may not rank as high as the "social debt" owed to the present generation. In general, poorer people have greater incentive to give priority to the immediate economic and social dimensions of sustainability rather than the longer-term environmental dimension because the perceived rationality of one's choice depends on both one's basic preferences among the dimension of sustainability and on one's immediate necessities.[5]

The existence of such variations in necessities, concepts, and circumstances means that a "one size fits all" approach to evaluation sustainable development is inappropriate. A group evaluating sustainable development must therefore determine what they mean by sustainable development, their purpose for evaluating it, and the circumstances in which they are working. With this foundation, they can design and implement the evaluation project, as they deem appropriate.

Why Evaluate Sustainable Development?

There are numerous reasons for evaluating efforts surrounding sustainable development, the following are a few:

- Analyze necessities
- Assure proper planning
- Assess progress relative to objectives
- Determine what has been achieved
- Identify strengths and weaknesses of the collective vision
- Assess effectiveness
- Assess efficiency
- Analyze costs
- Analyze benefits
- Facilitate continuous improvement
- Make wiser decisions
- Assess and/or allocate resources
- Identify needed training to develop adequate expertise
- Justify efforts, projects, and programs
- Determine policies and strategies
- Develop new knowledge
- Determine constraints
- Assess risk
- Report performance and results to funding sources
- Satisfy mandates (by government and/or other entities)
- Enhance public relations

The reasons and agendas behind specific evaluation projects can be as numerous and different as the interests, necessities, and circumstances of the people behind the evaluations. For example, one group may be interested in finding ways to protect or recover a cultural heritage; whereas another group may be interested in identifying factors that are offending their ecosystem and how to protect the options embodied within the system for present and for future generations.

People need the opportunity to determine and appreciate their reasons for evaluating a given effort in sustainable development in order to proceed appropriately. Some of the reasons for evaluation may not be obvious or easily understood by all citizens. Any person may see one or more reasons to evaluate a given project and not see other equally valid reasons. It is thus critical for all stakeholders to work together in articulating and clarifying their reasons for conducting an evaluation.

Without evaluation, one can neither tell the kind of contribution a given activity is making with respect to sustainability nor the extent to which one is progressing toward a stated goal, as Rachel Carson noted more than two decades ago. Carson lamented that the "contemporary society seldom evaluates the risk of a new technology before it is embedded in a vast economic and political commitment, becoming virtually impossible to alter."[6]

One premise of sustainable development is—and must be—an appropriate system of evaluation that enables citizens to understand the situation in which they are operating, figure out whether they need to change the situation, determine what questions to ask in the process, and find the answers. If, for instance, a community is wondering whether to initiate or maintain a given project, it is appropriate for the community to assess the need for and feasibility of the project by examining their vision, goals, and objectives. If it is determined that the project is necessary, the community needs to identify how best to proceed (for example, address the need to monitor progress over time in order to determine effectiveness, evaluate outcomes, and so on).

Evaluation of sustainable development systematically examines where things are headed and how, in order to understand whether they are moving in the desired direction. In this sense, evaluation is like balancing a checkbook. If one does not continually examine one's addition and subtraction, one might have to work backward through many entries to find an error when the total on the monthly bank statement is out of concert with that in one's checkbook. Once the error is found, the entire number of entries made since that time must be corrected in order to balance the checkbook with the monthly statement.

While correcting errors in one's checkbook is simply linear mathematics, nothing in life, other than our thinking, is linear, which means that each error we create in life sets into motion a chain of events that alters all subsequent conditions through time. If, therefore, one waits too long to check for errors, it will likely be too late to correct them once they are found because all of the potential circumstances will have changed through events set in motion by commission of the original error. With respect to sustainability, an evaluation is specifically designed to help people maintain a constant vigil and warn them in case of danger, such as straying from a desired course.

Such an evaluation requires giving people a leading voice in their destiny through active participation. Participatory evaluation empowers people to determine and control what is to be evaluated by enabling them to work together in defining and meeting their needs, beginning with the crafting of a shared vision of sustainable development.[7]

2

DEVELOPING A PLAN
FOR THE EVALUATION

Crafting a carefully worded vision and attendant goals that state clearly and concisely your desired future condition is the necessary first step in evaluation because it defines what you want from which you can extrapolate, what you think the journey will be like. Visions and goals are generally not designed to be measured. An objective, on the other hand, is dramatically different from a vision and goals, in that it is specifically designed to be measured within a defined time frame.

Objectives, in their turn, describe how one proposes to reach a particular goal within a specific time frame on the way to fulfilling one's vision. In the collective, one's vision, attendant goals, and their objectives form the context of the journey against which all decisions, actions, and consequences are measured (evaluated) to see if in fact the proposed journey is even possible as imagined and what the consequences of the journey might be.

Another reason a shared community vision and its attendant goals are important is that they build on and extend continuity of the community's history. What happens to one's sense of truth, reality, place, and community when the continuity of one's historical context is disregarded through seemingly random development? Destroying the history of a community through visionless development is to simultaneously destroy its memory, which in turn destroys the sense of history, trust, and place—the very essence of community.[8]

Start by finding out what people feel they need and are concerned about in a general sense. Make sure that everyone is genuinely encouraged and given a real opportunity to contribute to the discussion and visioning process. Use whatever sessions and techniques are necessary to generate a comprehensive list of issues people are interested in and then develop the group's vision, goals, and preliminary objectives by focusing on what is really important to the entire community.

Brainstorming, nominal group process—listening, listening, listening, and listening some more, as well as a community survey are a few techniques that may be used. Brainstorming involves the participants in thinking creatively outside of the "socially constructed box" and contributing their ideas without second-guessing either how silly they may sound or what their utility might be. Nominal group process allows people to express their "individual priorities" as best they can in the beginning and then moves to "group priorities." An additional community survey can provide large numbers of people with an opportunity to state their true opinion about an issue or subject of interest from the perceived safety of their homes.

Once a community has completed its statement of vision, goals, and preliminary objectives, it can answer the following questions concisely: (1) What do we (the people of this community) want? (2) Why do we want it? (3) Where do we want it? (4) When do we want it? (5) From whom do we want it? (6) How much (or how many) do we want? (7) For how long do we want it (or them)? If a component is missing, the community may achieve its desire by accident or serendipity, but not by design.

Only when the people can answer all of these questions concisely do they know where they want to go and the value of going there, and only then can they calculate the probability of arrival. Next, they must determine the cost, make the commitment to bear it, and resolve to keep their commitment.

Focusing the Evaluation

Focusing the evaluation includes (among other things) a preliminary inventory to understand the situation in which one is working. With this understanding, one can frame the evaluation objectives, discern important questions to ask, select variables and indicators to assess, and choose an approach or general framework for the evaluation project.[9]

Inventory

A preliminary inventory is a careful assessment of what exists at present and allows one to understand the circumstances with which one begins. Taking "inventory" represents the key to a successful evaluation for two reasons: (1) people need to understand the situation in which they are working before they can determine the relevancy of specific questions to the proposed evaluation, and (2) taking stock of the present situation is essential to planning the future, as well as appreciating any changes that may occur.

In turn, taking inventory requires the following questions: What exists now, before anything is purposefully altered? What condition is it in, and what is the prognosis for its future? Even though a preliminary evaluation may require multiple questions, the outcome is still a single realization.

If, for example, you visit your new doctor for an initial annual checkup, the doctor would have to take a series of measurements, such as your temperature, blood pressure, and blood tests in order to judge your current condition and make a prognosis for your future. If you are indeed healthy, then all is well; if not, your doctor may prescribe further tests to pinpoint what is wrong and ultimately some treatment to correct your ailment. Thus the initial baseline information provides a necessary benchmark against which the doctor can compare measurement taking later on to check on any changes on your health condition. But this requires knowing exactly what to evaluate.

Framing the Evaluation

Properly framing the objectives of an evaluation requires people to agree on and clearly articulate what they want to evaluate and why. It is important when framing an objective to keep the ideas simple and communicate them clearly in order to enhance understanding among all interested parties of why a given activity, project, or program must be evaluated. Further, objectives must be specific, measurable, attainable, reliable, and time-bound (SMART). It is equally important that people have a realistic and balanced expectation regarding what they can and cannot accomplish with evaluation.

Framing an objective calls for the ability to delineate a project or issue in order to measure it, while at the same time maintaining focus on the interconnectedness embodied in sustainable development through systems thinking. For instance, it must be recognized that the Greek word *oikos,* which means "house," is the shared root of both ecology and economy, where ecology is the knowledge or understanding of the house and economy is the management of the house—and it's the same house.

In addition, framing an objective requires both the ability to recognize the imperfections of the tools one uses, such as statistics and neoclassical economics, and the ability to creatively transcend their limitations. It is precisely the limitations of our tools that make the questions we ask and the indicators we choose so very important.[10]

Asking Relevant Questions

Asking relevant questions is a critical part of evaluation. Learning how to frame good and effective questions is paramount not only for crafting a collective vision for the future but also for the process of evaluating what is necessary to achieve the vision. A question is a powerful tool when used wisely because questions open the door of possibility. For example, it was not possible to go to the moon until someone asked: "Is it possible to go to the moon?" At that moment, going to the moon became a possibility. To be effective, each question must: (1) have a specific purpose, (2) contain a single idea, (3) be clear in meaning, (4) stimulate thought, (5) require a definite answer to bring closure to the human relationship induced by the question, and (6) explicitly relate to previous information.

A question that focuses on "right" versus "wrong" is thus a hopeless exercise because it calls for human moral judgment, and that is not a valid question to ask of either an ecosystem or science. With respect to science, author Layton K. Caldwell observes that, "the problem of applying science is not primarily a matter of knowledge, but of public will. . . ." If, on the other hand, one asked if a proposed action was good or bad in terms of a community's collective vision, that is a good question.

For example, a good short-term economic decision may simultaneously be a bad long-term ecological decision and thus a bad long-term economic decision. To find out, however, one must ask: Although this is a good short-term economic decision, is it also a good long-term ecological decision and hence a good long-term economic decision? An answer to anything is possible only when the question has been asked.

In essence, questions lead to the array of options from which one can choose. Conversely, without a question, one is blind to the options. Learning about the options is the purpose of an evaluation. In turn, to know what to evaluate and how to go about it, one must know what questions to ask because an answer is only meaningful and useful if it is in response to the right question.

If for example the objective of an evaluation is to solve a problem, some questions to consider are: What is the problem? Whose problem is it? What are the options for solving the problem? What new problems will solving the old one create? Who will benefit most and how from solving the problem? Who will be harmed most and how by solving the problem? When everything is considered, how will the solution affect the sustainability of the community?

If you want to evaluate the implementation of a project on the ground, the following question would be in order: Did we do what we said we were going to do? Although this type of evaluation is really just documentation of what was done, it is critical documentation because without it, it may not be possible to figure out what went awry (if anything did), how or why it went awry, or how to remedy it. Thus, to continue the doctor analogy, it is important to determine if the patient actually got the "treatment" the doctor ordered. Obviously, failure to implement the prescribed treatment appropriately can alter a variety of things, such as the patient's outcome and the doctor's interpretation of the outcome. Also, any doubt as to whether the prescribed treatment was implemented appropriately will seriously obscure the results.

To evaluate effectiveness, one must ask questions that determine how successful a given action was in achieving the objective. Returning to the doctor analogy, assessing effectiveness asks: Did the treatment work? In other words, did it perform as it was supposed to? Answering this question requires that the objective be specific, measurable, and time-bound. It also requires that the treatment or action plan be implemented appropriately, and that the results be clearly recognized.

Validating an outcome involves testing the assumptions that went into the development of the objectives and the models they are based on, which may require asking such questions as: Did the results come out as expected? If not, why not? What does this mean with respect to our conceptual model of how we think the system works versus how the system actually works? Will altering our approach make any difference in the outcome? If not, why not? If so, how and why? What target corrections do we need to make?

Identifying Variables

Identifying the variables is the next item in planning an evaluation. It involves the following steps:

1. Define the questions to be addressed in the evaluation and write them down simply and clearly.

2. Identify the important variables in each question and write them down.

3. Develop brief but clear definitions for each variable identified.

4. State any hypothesis about these variables with regard to the question encompassed in the evaluation. A hypothesis is a statement of what one thinks the answers to one's evaluation questions will be. A hypothesis can be developed from previous studies, experience, or logical reasoning.

5. Identify the specific kinds of information (indicators) necessary to measure or track each variable (identified in the second step above) in order to answer questions that compose the body of the evaluation.

Choosing Indicators

Indicators provide information (data) with which to assess whether one is in fact headed toward the attainment of a desired condition (the condition of a community's collective vision), maintaining the current condition, or moving away from the desired condition. A good indicator helps a community recognize potential problems and provides insight into possible solutions. What a community chooses to measure, how it measures it, and how it interprets and uses the results will have a tremendous effect on their social, economic, and ecological sustainability.

It is therefore critical that a community choose good indicators to tell them what is happening with respect to their stated objectives. Choosing indicators wisely is based on addressing such issues as the meaning of sustainability and how to tell if the object being monitored (say, an institution, community, or project) is in fact operating in a sustainable manner.[11]

Indicators are pivotal elements of information that, when studied over time, point to changes (if any) in the variables a community is concerned with. Indicators thus reflect collective values because they help: (1) build consensus around the goals, (2) sharpen the objectives, (3) evaluate the effect of specific actions, and (4) demonstrate progress to the citizens.

Indicators must relate directly to a community's stated objectives for the evaluation and must be tailored to the scope and scale of what the community wants to accomplish. Put differently, indicators must be customized with respect to: (1) the people's interest, (2) the relevant area of consideration, and (3) the selected time frame. For the purpose of choosing appropriate indicators with which to measure sustainability, it is important to ask the following questions:

- What are we interested in sustaining?
- Over what period of time (temporal scale) do we want to sustain it?
- What physical area (spatial scale) must be accounted for, given the processes to be used, as well as those to be measured, the number and kind(s) of process elements involved, and the type of human interest involved?

It is imperative that people understand the pivotal role of scale in the assessment of sustainability in order to figure out the appropriate temporal and spatial scale for their indicators. Authors C. Lee Campbell and Walter W. Heck discussed the importance of scales in the measurement of ecological sustainability this way:

> Temporal and spatial scales are key elements in assessing ecosystem integrity. The temporal scale must be sufficiently

long to identify what the "normal" state of the ecosystem should be and to determine whether departures from "normal" are indeed trends or mere random variations. Long-term observations are needed to reveal slow changes in a system component that would be viewed as constant with short-term observations. Similarly, observations made on a large scale may reveal heterogeneity not apparent from limited local observations.[12]

Good indicators of sustainable development must reflect something basic and fundamental to the long-term economic, social, or environmental health of a community over generations. To select indicators of such quality requires the following criteria:

- must be recognizable, clear, and simple
- can be understood and accepted by the community
- are quantifiable
- are sensitive to change across space and time or within groups
- are predictive or anticipatory
- operate on values represented by discernible reference points or thresholds
- reveal the extent to which changes are reversible and controllable
- data are relatively easy to collect and use
- qualitatively, the methodologies used to develop an indicator must be clearly defined, accurately described, socially and scientifically acceptable, and easily reproduced
- must be sensitive to time, which means an indicator measured annually can show representative trends[13]

Indicators close the circle of action by both allowing and demanding that a community come back to its beginning premise and ask (reflect on) whether, because of the actions and other contextual factors, the community is better off now than when it started: If so, how? If not, why? If not, can the situation be remedied? If so, how? If not, why? And so on.

Here a caution is necessary. Using only one indicator or measuring only one aspect of sustainability (for example, economy) ignores the complex relationships among economy, community, environment, neighboring communities, and the Bioregion. When each component is viewed as a separate issue and thus evaluated in isolation, the information tends to become skewed and leads to ineffective policies that, in turn, can lead to a deteriorating quality of life. If, for example, you go to your doctor but only allow her or him to take your blood pressure without letting the doctor check your temperature, cholesterol level, and so on, the doctor cannot deal with your health as a systemic whole and thus loses the ability to see the various components as parts of an interdependent and integrated system. In this, your body is similar in principle and function to your family, the community in which your family resides, the landscape in which your community rests, and the landscape within the Bioregion. This notion is exemplified by the writings of Rachel Carson, who says, in her book *Silent Spring,* something that still rings true: "This is an era of specialists [and growing more so], each of whom sees his [or her] own problem and is unaware of, or intolerant of, the larger frame into which it fits."[14]

We therefore need to use a variety of indicators in order to capture the many dimensions of whatever is being evaluated if a community is to have any kind of accurate assessment of its sustainable well-being. Only with enough relevant indicators and a systematic way of tracking them is it possible to make a prognosis for the future based on the collective vision, its attendant goals, and the operational objectives. And only by systematically tracking all the important indicators is it possible to make the necessary target corrections to achieve the community's vision because only now does the community know which corrections to make.

Development of good indicators for measuring sustainability requires full participation by all interested citizens. For local communities, that means extensive community participation involving all interested parties to: (1) agree on the objectives, (2) generate a long list of potential indicators with input from a cross-section of the community, and (3) use a participatory (sometimes iterative) process to select a reasonable number of functional indicators from the list of possibilities.

To summarize, people need to make a participatory decision on what to evaluate and why based on such things as: information needed by interested parties, group priorities, available resources, budget, time, skill, and feasibility. In other words, after developing a comprehensive list of needed information, they have to decide what questions they really want to ask as a group. Since individual members of a given group will likely have different ideas regarding these issues, participants should be encouraged to put all their ideas on the table (so everyone will know the individual expectations people have) in order to develop a group expectation and a common vision for conducting the evaluation. Active participation of everyone involved is necessary to avoid confusion about where the group wants to go, how to get there, and know when it has arrived.

One way to accomplish the above is for skilled facilitator(s) to lead the group through a discussion or planning process to do the following:

1. Craft a collective vision based on consensus about the desired future.

2. Clearly define the purpose of the evaluation.

3. Clearly frame the questions the evaluation is meant to find answers for.

4. Identify the information (data) needed to answer the questions pertaining to the evaluation through the careful selection specific variables (indicators) associated with each question. This may include things to be measured, observed, monitored, and so on.

5. Discuss the need for each piece of information (data) to insure that all necessary information is collected and only necessary information is collected.

Transformative facilitation can be used to generate ideas and arrive at group consensus at each of the above steps.[15] To be effective, however, the facilitation must be done correctly as the following stories illustrate.

One of us (Ukaga) observed a Participatory Rural Appraisal[16] activity in a little village near Pune, India, where an individual who was supposed to facilitate a team activity simply did not know how to yield control of the evaluation process to the local villagers. Without asking for the villagers' ideas of what their perceived needs and desires were, this fellow took over and started telling the villagers what he thought they should do. He was reminded that we were not there to tell the people what we thought needed to be done, but rather to facilitate the villagers' own process of what *they thought* they wanted to do.

"Yes, I am just facilitating," was his response, after which he proceeded to tell the villagers, all of whom were now sitting on the floor of their town hall, what the objective of their evaluation should be. Again, he was reminded that he should not be dictating to the people, who by now were listening passively.

"Yes, yes," he said, "I know that I should let them do it by themselves, but I just want to tell them what to do," and again proceeded to instruct the villagers how to conduct the evaluation. It was only after whispering to him a third time that he needed to turn the meeting over to the people and let them determine some of these things by themselves that he said, "yes, participation, yes" and appropriately turned the process over to the people.

As one might imagine, the villagers came alive as soon as they were given the chance to determine what to do and how to do it. They became invigorated and exhibited great wisdom, skill, experience, and expertise in identifying and assessing things that are most important to them—factors that only moments before were not even recognized or talked about.

Beginning with an 85-year-old man who gave the history of the village, the people provided important information, asked questions, challenged assumptions, identified problems and opportunities. Rather than sitting passively in the town hall listening to someone else, and perhaps answering a few questions, the people walked around their entire village, where they methodologically involved more people in the conversation as they worked to better understand their community. After much discussion, they reached a consensus on several things, including their objectives.

Although some of us understandably have to work hard to counter our tendency to keep control, it is not simply a matter of knowing what to do because our behavioral patterns, which may contradict our intellectual knowledge, are often unconscious. In addition, the people in the audience may appear comfortable in their passive role, such as sitting and listening to someone tell them what needs to be done. Be not misled by such appearances, however; people need to take control of their destiny and will, if given a voice. In this sense, simplicity is the watchword.

In contrast to the individual Ukaga observed in India, Maser (the second author) outlined a simple process for the citizens to follow and then acted simply as a facilitator to keep the process on track when he worked in northwestern California, where the citizens wanted to develop a vision for the future of their small community. The community hosted a one-day conference that began with a panel composed of two families—grandparents, parents, and three or four children ages eight to sixteen.

The grandparents began by telling the audience and one another what the community had been like in their day, what they had liked most about it, what they had liked least about it, the significant changes they had seen, and how they had felt about them. Then came the parents' turn to go navigate the same journey down memory lane. Finally, the children spoke, but theirs was a view in the present tense of how they saw their community today, what they liked most about it, liked least about it, what they would change if they could, the significant changes they had seen over which they had no control, and how they had felt about them. The differences in tenses were not only stunning but also made the entire experience multi-dimensional in time and space, something neither members of the panel nor members of the audience had ever fully experienced before.

The result was half a day in which the residents of this tightly knit community listened to one another as they never had before and arrived at the conclusion that they had never really listened to what their children were trying to tell them, let alone ask their children what kind of community they wanted them—as parents—to create for them to live in. The children, in turn, felt safe in telling the adults what they wanted their community to be like when they grew up and had children of their own.

After lunch and following some instruction in the differences among a vision, goals, and objectives the people broke into five small groups to begin crafting their collective vision for the future of their community. It was wonderful to listen to parents for once ask the children what they wanted and really listening to them and taking seriously what they said.

Toward the evening, each group had selected a representative to present the individual group's effort to the conferees as a whole. Three of the groups had chosen children eight, nine, and eleven years old to present the findings—and they did a marvelous job. Finally, a second meeting was set to collate the ideas of the small groups into a collective straw vision for community comment. Again, the children were selected by the adults to represent them at the next work meeting, which would establish a straw vision and set the basis for long-term evaluation. This kind of behavior is what we mean by "participatory."

The whole process of evaluation must therefore be simple enough for all interested citizens to grasp, even children, which allows local people to maintain control of the entire process by actively participating in all stages thereof. Depending on the size, interest, and expertise of the citizen's group, it may be useful to form an evaluation team of technical experts and interested persons to facilitate and coordinate the effort. In any case, one needs the active participation of a broad coalition of individuals, organizations, and community representatives when dealing with the evaluation of sustainable development because the outcome will affect a broad spectrum of people in a variety of ways over time.

Whether working with a whole community or a smaller team, the first thing (at the first meeting) a facilitator or participant must do is ask, encourage, *and make it safe* for the people to define the issue(s) as they understand it, because a group's decision often emerges from the answers of individual people considered in the collective. Next, the facilitator or participant should then give an overview of the project or issue(s) the group is interested in to make sure everyone understands; then the people must be asked whether they understand the project and agree with its purpose. To this end, the following questions may be useful:

- What about the project requires evaluation, as you perceive it?
- What variables are related to the project or issue?
- Which ones rank as important?
- What events, incidents, or things are associated with the project in what degree of magnitude?
- Has a previous evaluation of this or a related project been done before?
- What is known about past and current efforts or strategies as they relate to the project?
- What do we want to find out or evaluate?

Depending on the nature of the project, the group may need people with expertise in certain fields, such as medicine, agriculture, engineering, sociology, or statistics to help provide and interpret specialized or technical information, thus allowing the people to make the best possible decisions regarding their evaluation project. In such situations, the intent must be for the "expert" to serve the people in helping them identify, define, and meet their needs—not for him or her to take over the process and thereby render the people passive participants. While data crunching and other technical aspects of evaluation are important, the part that deserves the most attention, we argue, is skillfully working with people to enable them to choose relevant and appropriate questions for their own evaluation process.

The participants must be given appropriate opportunities to use their experiences, expertise, and talents to address the issue at hand. Another important strategy is to have clear goal(s) for every meeting or activity. Once a group has agreed on what they want to evaluate and why (usually selected from a long list generated at initial brainstorming or planning sessions), the next step is to identify specific variables that relate to their objectives. Identifying specific variables is crucial to selecting key pieces of information (indicators) that, when studied, will reveal any change(s) in the variables and thus make it possible to answer the questions posed concerning the evaluation.

Participants can start this process by listing basic, easily understood questions to which they are interested in finding answers. Next, they must identify important variables in each question and develop brief definitions of those variables in order to specify the data they need to collect. Identifying the variables becomes a balancing act to ensure that all needed data are obtained while simultaneously assuring that no unnecessary data is collected. This calls for tough decisions that must involve all stakeholders or interested parties as they determine the data necessary to meet their stated evaluation objectives.

3

DATA COLLECTION

As with any study, there is a certain amount of work necessary prior to actual collection of data. Evaluating sustainable development is no different. Data collection typically entails choosing and using appropriate:

- Sources of data
- Population or sample size
- Methods of collecting data

Sources of Data

As discussed in the previous chapter, people involved in evaluation need to determine what kind of data they need to collect in order to generate the information necessary to meet their stated evaluation objectives. Then, they need to identify the best sources of the data as follows: (1) list specific pieces of data needed; (2) identify both primary and secondary sources for each piece of data in order to produce a comprehensive list of all potential sources from which to derive the required data; (3) consider the reliability, validity, feasibility, benefits, costs, and other relevant factors associated with each source of a needed piece of data; and (4) select the best source for getting the data needed to answer the questions relevant to the evaluation, which means accounting for the information in steps two and three above.

Choosing the right source(s) for each piece of data needed, requires paying close attention to a variety of factors such as asking which ones are the most valid and reliable, as well as the most feasible. The feasibility is determined by considering the available resources (for example, human, financial, technical, and time), as well as the politics, culture, and other contextual factors. For instance, a primary source of data, such as a first-hand account by an actual participant in an event, is preferable to a secondhand account because the former is generally more reliable than the latter—albeit more difficult to obtain.

One must always be careful to examine both primary and secondary sources of data to assure their authenticity, accuracy, and completeness. Against this background, it must be noted that a group may be limited in terms of the type and amount of data that are either readily available or can be collected. If, for any reason, the achievement of your evaluation objectives is likely to be limited by inadequate data, the objectives may need to be revised to make them more realistic. Alternatively, the choice may be made to either suspend the evaluation or make an extra effort to secure adequate data. If the decision is to proceed with data collection, the group must then decide whether to study the entire population of interest or to use a sample.[17]

Population or Sample

The entire aggregate of things, people, or objects of interest that one wants to study in a given evaluation is called a population.[18] When the entire population is studied, it is called a census. In some cases, however, it is not possible to study an entire population because of cost, practicality, time, human resources, and so on. Moreover, it is often unnecessary to study all the components of a population in order to know something about that population as a whole. If, for example, one wants to know how a bottle of wine tastes, a sip or perhaps a glass will do. It is unnecessary to drink all the wine to determine its flavor. Similarly, if one wants to learn something about a population, one can do so by examining sample items from that population.

The procedure whereby representative items from a population are selected in order to study and understand their characteristics, and then generalize back to the total population, is called sampling. The purpose of the evaluation (that is, description versus inference) will determine if the data is to be generalized to the population. Sampling allows evaluators to estimate properties of a population or test hypotheses about a particular population based on the study of a sufficient number of items selected from that population in question.

Types of Sampling

If one chooses to use a sample, one must also select a sample that is suitable for the given evaluation by reviewing the options and considering the pros and cons of using different types of sampling. Common types of sampling include purposive sampling, random sampling, systematic sampling, and cluster sampling.

Purposive sampling is where the elements of the population to be studied are selected based on the evaluator's purpose or judgment. This type of sampling is also called nonprobabilistic sampling because the individuals in the population will not have an equal chance or probability of being chosen for examination.

A sample of the first 100 farmers to adopt a certain water-saving irrigation system in a village would be an example of purposive sample. Obviously such a sample is not randomly selected from the population (village), which means that it might be biased. Nevertheless, it may be exactly what is needed if a group is interested in studying early adopters of such a practice in that particular village. Thus, purposeful sample can be very useful, effective, and efficient in yielding answers to important questions, especially in a qualitative evaluation.

Purposeful sampling must be based on the evaluator's informed idea of who has the information needed or other relevant factors, however, and not mere convenience. For instance, following the September 11, 2001, bombing of the World Trade Center and the subsequent discovery of anthrax in certain places in the United States, it made sense to examine all the individuals and locations directly and indirectly connected to the known cases of anthrax in order to fully understand and solve the problem, rather than studying all locations in the entire country, or world for that matter.

Simple random sampling involves selecting a sample in a way that gives all members of the defined population, say the citizens of a community, an equal and independent chance of being selected as part of the sample. For each member of a given population to have the same probability of being chosen, the list of all members in that population must be complete and current; in other words, everybody in the community must have his or her name on the list.

Random sampling can be accomplished in a variety of ways. One of the simplest ways is by writing the name of each and every member in the population on individual pieces of paper, putting these in a container, mixing them up, and randomly drawing one individual at a time to be included in the sample until the desired sample size is reached. If, for instance, one wanted to get a simple random sample of 30 individuals out of a population of 150 people, this could be done by writing the name of each of these 150 persons on a piece of paper, putting these papers in a hat, mixing them up to give each person equal chance of being chosen, and then drawing names from the hat at random until the desired sample size of individuals is reached. For all the individuals to truly have equal chance, however, drawn names are supposed to be put back into the hat before subsequent drawings. Other common ways of sampling are by using a *random number table* or *random number generator*. These are particularly useful when, for reasons such as population size, sampling methods like "drawing from the hat" would not work as easily.

Stratified random sampling involves sorting out a population based on pertinent factors, such as those people in a population who are for growth and those in the same population who are against it. Each discrete group—growth versus no growth—is considered to be a "subpopulation" of the community as a whole. If growth versus no growth were the only division in a community, then the population would be made up of two subpopulations. A community, however, will most probably have more than two subpopulations based on differences, such as gender, age, socio-economic factors, political affiliation, and so on.

Once the population of the community as a whole has been divided into mutually exclusive categories that are appropriate, meaningful, and relevant in the context of the given evaluation, it is said to be stratified—just like different layers of a cake. Then, one can randomly choose members of each subpopulation or stratum in order to assure that all important aspects of the population as a whole are captured, which is much like making sure to taste each layer of a cake randomly taking a bite out of each layer to determine as accurately as possible how the cake as a whole tastes without getting sick by eating the whole thing. Making sure that identified subpopulations are represented in the sample in proportion to their relative size is called a proportional stratified random sampling. Systematic sampling entails numbering every individual member of the population and choosing every n^{th} member for inclusion in the sample. For instance, if one wants to interview a sample of individuals living in a given village using systematic sampling, one can get or make a list of all the residents and then select for interview every n^{th} person on the list. This means selecting every 5th person (5th, 10th, 15th, and so on) if one decides to make "n" equal to 5. If "n" is to equal 9, every 9th person on the list would be selected. The value of "n" can be determined by dividing the size of the population by size of the desired sample.

It is important to note that, with systematic sampling, all members of the population do not have an independent chance of being selected for the sample because members to be included in are determined automatically once the first member is selected. While a systematic sample can be considered a random sample if the list from which members are being selected is ordered at random, randomly ordered lists are seldom available in reality. Further, it may be impractical to list and number all members of a given population in order to sample it systematically. For this reason, systematic sampling is generally inferior, with regard to representation, as a sampling technique when compared with random sampling.

Cluster sampling involves choosing elements or subjects to be studied from a population in groups called clusters rather than on an individual basis. For example, instead of selecting individuals at random from a list of community residents, one can choose a number of families and then study everyone belonging to each family. A family is considered a cluster in this case because it is an intact group, such as the Johnsons or the Ukagas.

Sampling several intact groups (clusters) and studying all the elements within the chosen clusters can be used when a complete picture (a list and stratification of all the members) of the population as a whole is not available. Cluster sampling is particularly useful when working with a large or highly dispersed population or one that cannot be conveniently sampled on an individual basis. Further, it is generally less expensive, less time consuming, and easier for some to understand than either random sampling or stratified random sampling. But, it may not be as effective. Steps in cluster sampling include:

- Defining the population
- Determining the sample size
- Identifying the clusters
- Compiling a list of clusters that comprise the population
- Estimating the average size of a cluster

- Determining the number of clusters needed to achieve the desired sample size
- Randomly selecting the needed number of clusters
- Including all the members of the selected clusters in the sample

Suppose you want to study the lifestyles of people who live on rural lake properties in Minnesota using the cluster sampling method. You would define the population or group that is the focus of your study and determine how much sample of the population you need for your study. Then, taking all the properties around one lake as a cluster, you can compile a list of all lakes in the target area and estimate the average number of people living on each lake. Next, you would divide the required sample size by the average number of people on a lake to get the number of clusters needed to achieve the sample size. Finally, you would select that number of lakes at random and study everyone living on the selected lakes.

Sample Size

A sample that is too small limits one's ability to understand the population being evaluated and one that is unnecessarily large can be overly expensive without adding materially to the information being sought. Thus, the idea is to use a sample size that truly answers the questions being asked about a given population without spending extra money, time, or other resources unnecessarily.

Suppose you want to know something about the residents of a village. Assuming that the population consists of 1000 individuals, how many would one need to study in order to draw a general inference about the population as a whole? Obviously, a sample of one would be too small for much understanding with respect to the entire population of the village. On the other hand, a sample of 999 individuals would be more than necessary to glean the needed information about the village. What, therefore, would the appropriate sample size be? The answer depends among other things on the purpose of the study, the size of the population, the margin of error one is willing to accept, and the homogeneity of the population.

Thus, appropriate sample sizes for experimental studies can be estimated using statistical techniques that account for such important factors as: (1) probability that the sample(s) will be representative of the population (*confidence level*), (2) the extent to which means of samples drawn repeatedly from the population differ from one another and seemingly from the population mean (*sampling error*), and (3) proportional representation in the sample of each population category on important parameters (in *stratified sampling*).[19]

With qualitative evaluation, as opposed to the quantitative evaluation discussed above, the adequacy of a sample may not be determined statistically. Instead, a sample is considered adequate when saturation of data is reached—meaning that such a sample would yield the level of information needed to clearly understand and describe the phenomenon being investigated. Further, the appropriateness of a sample in qualitative or naturalistic evaluation should be determined by the extent to which the evaluator(s) are able to gather the necessary data to provide the required information about that which is being evaluated.

If necessary, the participants should use experts to help them make well-informed decisions regarding questions around sampling, such as:

1. Should we use a population or sample?
2. If so, what type of sampling should we use?
3. How much (sample size) is adequate?

Also, a person with expertise in sampling can help the group identify and deal with potential bias in their proposed sampling design.

Sample Bias

Sampling bias can result from a variety of factors, such as using: (1) an inadequately defined population; (2) atypical samples, for example, volunteers who may be more interested or motivated about a project than nonvolunteers, which would introduce a bias because the entire population consists both of volunteers and nonvolunteers, each of whom may differ somewhat; and (3) infrequently selected subpopulations without assurance that they adequately represent the larger population, which makes it difficult or impossible to discover generalized information about a given subpopulation with respect to the population as a whole.

Therefore, people involved in evaluation must be conscious of sampling bias and do their best to avoid it. Specific ways to avoid such bias include:

- Making sure the characterization of the population is accurate and complete

- Being conscious of the fact that official boundaries may not reflect pertinent factors of sustainability, such as differences among ecological processes, cultural biases, distinctive features of a landscape, carrying capacity of a community, and so on

- Giving adequate training to those who will conduct the evaluation

- Allocating sufficient time, money, personnel, and other resources to complete the project in a quality fashion

- Avoiding the temptation to use a biased sample simply because it is convenient to do so

If sampling bias is unavoidable, the evaluator(s) must recognize and acknowledge this, as well as its implication for the results of the given evaluation. Such honesty will help the users decide for themselves how serious the bias is and to what extent they believe it might have affected the results.

Assuming that the required information has been clearly specified, the best sources of data have been chosen, the population or sample type and size to use has been determined, as well as how to avoid bias, one is ready to begin actual collection of data.

Options for Collecting Data

Anyone engaged in the evaluation of sustainable development has a variety of options for collecting data. Group processes (for example, brainstorming, focus group, nominal group process, etc.), content analysis, community meeting, surveys, creative expressions, diaries/journals/logs, interviewing, investigative inquiry, mapping, observation, pilot projects, photography, scales, stories/testimonials/anecdotes, workshops, tests and measurements, records, field notes, unobtrusive methods, and community study are some examples.

Brainstorming involves participants in thinking creatively to stimulate ideas. Because there are *only ideas* in brainstorming (no bad ideas), participants can be encouraged to speak up quickly, which often stimulates others to think more creatively than they might do otherwise. Incorporating ideas from each participant or each small group of participants in a general discussion stretches their imagination and encourages self-expression.

A focus group is a special type of group interview or organized discussion that may be used "to gain a deeper understanding of participants' views and experiences, their feelings, perceptions, beliefs, knowledge, and attitudes about the topic being investigated."[20] Many issues, such as quality of life, protection of natural resources and ecosystems, patterns of consumption, toxic pollution, global climate change, and so on, that concern people in various communities can be good topics for focus groups.

Nominal group process allows people to express their "individual priorities" in the beginning and then move from there to "group priorities." It is therefore a powerful tool for collecting data based on group judgment, as opposed to individual opinions. One way to do this is for the participants to: (1) introduce themselves, (2) do some ice-breakers, (3) introduce the subject or issue, (4) do a round-robin of ideas, (5) have group discussions on the subject, (6) reach a consensus or vote on the subject, (7) have a group discussion of the first vote, (8) determine the central message, and (9) wrap-up.

It is pertinent to note that there are differences among the various group processes with regard to when decisions are made and who makes decisions. In other words, different group processes are useful for different purposes. For instance, brainstorming and focus groups are generally used for data gathering only, since the decisions are made after the group. Whereas with nominal and Delphic groups, in addition to generating data, the decisions are made as part of the process by the group.

Content analysis involves a careful examination and systematic description of the components of existing materials (for example, documents) as they relate to a proposed evaluation.

Community meetings provide a forum for discussing the subject of an evaluation, listening to others, presenting findings and ideas, critiquing group judgments, and reaching collective decisions.

A community survey can be used to provide a large number of people with the opportunity to express their opinions about an issue or subject of interest to their community. It must be noted, however, that people's attitudes and perceptions can differ from reality. Nevertheless, a community survey can enable respondents to think about both past and present conditions of their community, as well as what they want to improve and to what extent they are willing to support such improvements.

Creative expression, such public art, storytelling, and music can be used as a means of individual or group expression, as well as for collecting, documenting, and interpreting data.

Diaries, journals, and logs are useful for individual or group records of relevant events and activities, as well as personal reflections about thoughts, feelings, expectations, misgivings, interpretations, and other important impressions.

Interviewing, which is a communication process and can be carefully structured, semi-structured, or informal conversation, provides an opportunity for the evaluator to gather pertinent information. While interviews can generate in-depth data in ways that questionnaires or surveys cannot, they tend to be relatively time consuming, labor intensive, and costly, especially with large samples. Interviewing also requires good skills with communication and interpersonal relationships, which can pose a problem for data collectors who lack these skills. Strategies for conducting good interviews include:

- Making sure the interviewer is well trained and able to conduct an interview appropriately

- Using some type of interview schedule or written material as a guide in asking initial and follow-up questions

- Using the first few minutes to develop good interpersonal relations with the interviewee before broaching the questions

- Clarifying the purpose of the interview and specific questions as necessary

- Assuring confidentiality of responses—especially with sensitive or personal information

- Skillfully allowing respondents the flexibility to provide information, as they feel comfortable while simultaneously keeping the conversation focused to help an interviewee stay on-track

- Avoid doing or saying any thing that might disturb or upset the respondent

- Avoiding leading questions

- Maintaining a neutral and professional demeanor throughout the interview

- Recording responses accurately

Investigative inquiry, which is traditionally used by journalists to expose situations of wrongdoing, can be adapted in an evaluation to determine the reason a given phenomenon has taken place, whatever it might be.

Mapping is the graphic representation by the citizens of their community or the subject of their evaluation, which is a useful tool for eliciting, recording, and comparing data, such as the pre- and post-event perceptions of participants.

Observation, which can be obtrusive or unobtrusive, involves seeing, listening, tasting and/or otherwise experiencing or capturing the phenomenon that is being evaluated. As the name implies, data collection relies on an evaluators' observation, unlike self-report methods, such as interviews and surveys. Here, observation is used in a broad sense to include what is seen, heard, felt, smelled, and so on.

There are many methods of collecting data unobtrusively, such as using how worn the carpet in a hallway is to assess or determine how much traffic goes through it and, by implication, how well it is used; or quietly observing or using electronic devices to unobtrusively collect data about something one is interested in studying, without asking people or letting them know. In evaluation of sustainable development, unobtrusive observation can be particularly useful in cases where people's awareness of being observed may cause them to behave differently and thus yield misleading or unrealistic data. Yet, even in such cases, unobtrusive methods must be chosen carefully, done legally, and used with caution and sensitivity to protect people's privacy and trust.

A pilot project can serve as a trial or test that yields information for future decisions or steps based on data collected. Pilot projects allow the testing of an idea on a small scale to make sure it works before going further, which is critical when failure of a full-scale project may have very costly environmental or social consequences.

Photography, which can be still frames, motion pictures in black and white or color, digital, or otherwise, provides a visual record of events; activities; and/or the current or past situation of thing, project, process, or outcome. As the saying goes, a picture is worth more than a thousand words because it can capture things, such as emotions and context, that words cannot touch with any sense of reality.

Scales, which can be written, graphic, or verbal descriptors, are used to rank the characteristics of that which is being evaluated, such as categories (sustainable versus nonsustainable) or a continuum (highly sustainable, sustainable, neutral, nonsustainable, or highly nonsustainable).

Stories and testimonials, which can be oral, written, audio taped, or video taped accounts of past and present situations or future projections, can be a useful source of information about the subject of interest, or as a basis for discussions, as well as data generation and analysis.

Models, as concise description or representation of reality, can be powerful tools with which an entire system or a specific part of the system can be examined under different conditions. A model is a simplified representation of reality that aims to capture the most important features of that which is being studied, but without all the complications of its so-called "less significant" details. Models can also be used as a guide to better identify a problem, as well as collect and analyze data necessary to its understanding and solution.

A model may first be constructed in a preliminary or partial form to identify perceived critical aspects of the situation and the kind of data needed. It may then be elaborated and expanded under various scenarios as more is known about subject of study or about the community project or activity involved.

An example of the use of models, is a project we conducted in 2001 to explore options for electric energy production by the City of Grand Marias, Minnesota. This project involved a collaborative effort by the City, University of Minnesota, Institute for Sustainable Future, and local citizens to generate data necessary for the decision makers to choose method(s) of producing electricity that best suited the people. As part of this effort, a dynamic simulation model was created with data gathered from community meetings and secondary sources that allowed the comparison of costs and impacts (environmental, economic, and social) associated with a variety of strategies to produce and conserve energy. The model was then used to facilitate participatory discussions and informed decision making at subsequent community meetings.

Workshops provide a forum through which diverse elements of the community can interact concerning issues of mutual interest. Workshops can be used to generate and integrate rational and intuitive thinking; to build team consensus; and to generate creativity and energy among a group of people within a relatively short time. They can be used to collect data as well as to disseminate information and develop the citizens' concepts and skills with respect to community development. Essential ingredients for a successful workshop include: (1) enthusiasm; (2) participation; (3) demonstration, by which we mean playing a game of cards to show someone how the game is played or planting corn to show how corn is planted; and (4) a proper introduction of the workshop.[21]

Tests and Measurements involve the use of instruments, protocols, and standards to measure or test relevant subjects. For example, one can take various kinds of measurements to help collect data for answering such pertinent evaluation questions as: what is the number of people in this community; what is the weight of individuals in pounds, what is their height in feet, their age in years, and their food intake in calories per day? Similarly, we can measure other things, such as a community's soil erosion in tons per year, gasoline consumption in gallons per year, solid waste sent to the local landfill in tons per year, air pollutant emissions in tons per year, electricity use in mega watts per year, and so on.

A questionnaire is a set of written questions used to elicit information either by having respondents complete the questionnaire, usually in writing, but also verbally, or by using the questionnaire as a guide for personal telephone interviews. The people involved should be able to: (1) select the best instruments if they decide to use or adapt ready-made ones, and (2) construct the best instrument for their purpose, if they need to develop their own.

There are several things to look for when choosing an instrument, such as evidence of validity. An instrument is considered valid for a given purpose if it measures completely what it is supposed to measure and nothing else. For example, one would use a thermometer to measure temperature and a scale to measure weight—not a thermometer.

The validity of instruments, such as questionnaires, that generate data by asking questions and getting responses (as opposed to direct measurement or observation) depend, among other things, on the cooperation of respondents, such as telling the truth and being aware of the information the evaluator is after, and so on. With this in mind, evaluators should check each question in a questionnaire to make sure that: (1) it does not ask for information the respondent would not be able to provide, (2) it is not likely to generate a socially acceptable answer, and (3) that it would not lead respondents to anticipate what the evaluator wants to hear and try to respond accordingly.

The goal in designing an instrument, beyond the assurance of its validity, is to assure its reliability. An instrument's reliability can be compromised by sources of random error in measurements, such as errors in scoring, errors due to guessing, and errors caused by inherent fluctuations in an instrument's precision.

It is advisable, therefore, to select standardized instruments that fit the prescribed purpose and are accompanied by evidence of validity, reliability, and clear directions on: (1) how to use the instrument, (2) how to record the measurements, and (3) how to interpret findings. If, however, an appropriate ready-made instrument is not available, the people who are going to do the evaluation may have to develop their own instrument.

The service of a skilled consultant, professional staff, or volunteer may be needed if required expertise is not available among the citizens themselves. Such an expert can work with the citizens to identify and examine instruments that are available and help them select and adapt the best instrument for their work. And if an appropriate one cannot be found, the person can assist the citizens in developing a custom-made instrument for their project.

Records are a valuable source of data and very important when dealing with information that is easily forgotten. In keeping records for purposes of monitoring and evaluation, careful consideration should to be given to both the information to be recorded and the design of the recording forms. The goal is to assure that: (1) all the data necessary for answering the evaluation questions are recorded, (2) resources are not wasted collecting unnecessary additional information, and (3) recording forms and format allow for easy data entry, retrieval, analysis, interpretation, and so on. Further, recorded information should be regularly checked to insure that it is both complete and accurate.

Community study involves in-depth investigation of one or several areas of interest to a community by the citizenry itself. Rather than an "outsider" coming to reside in the community and interact with people in order to study them, the people are instead empowered to assess their own community by themselves. Since people generally trust data they help collect, community residents will act more readily upon information they discover themselves about their community than they would on information forwarded by outsiders. It is therefore important that local participants understand the basic tools and processes necessary for proper investigation in order to collect valid and reliable data that can provide them with a sound base on which to make decisions about their community. Participatory Rural Appraisal is one great variation of community study.

Participatory Rural Appraisal (PRA) refers to a growing family of approaches to evaluation that enable local people to collectively share and analyze their conditions, experiences, and knowledge and to plan and act accordingly.[22] Typically, PRA is a semi-structured systematic field activity carried out by a multi-disciplinary team to acquire information and formulate hypotheses for community development. It helps communities mobilize their human and natural resources, define problems, consider previous successes and challenges, and then prepare a systematic and site-specific plan of action that they can adopt and implement. Data collected through a Participatory Rural Appraisal includes: (1) secondary data, (2) spatial data, (3) time-related data, (4) social data, (5) institutional analysis, and (6) technical data.

Sources of *secondary data* include published and unpublished materials, other (nearby) projects, relevant reports, census data, maps, photographs, and satellite imagery. These data provide an initial overview of the area of interest through such general information as an area's resource base and management, land use, problems, opportunities, and past experiences in development. Although it is helpful to review available secondary data before beginning the fieldwork, one must avoid attempting to review all available secondary information, which can be overwhelming costly. One should, therefore, consider the information's relevance and cost in terms of time, money, and human resources, which means that only useful secondary information should be analyzed and summarized in simple graphs, tables, charts, and reports.

Spatial data refers to information, such as a sketch of a project site, map, and transect of the community of interest, which provide a powerful visual sense of the location and its various interrelationships. For instance, sketches of different farm households in a village may reveal variations in size, cultural practices, crops and animals raised, and so on. A transect gives a cross-sectional view of a community.

Typically, a Participatory Rural Appraisal team would walk across the area in a way that would allow them to capture as much of its specific characteristics and diversity as possible, including information gathered through casual interviews of people met along the way. These characteristics are then represented graphically.

Time-related data (for example, seasonal calendar of activities, timeline of past events) would highlight or reveal things that are important to local residents. For instance, *seasonal calendars* will show cycles or patterns of activities that occur within a community over a period of one year or so, while a *timeline* would reveal important events in the history of a community including past problems and achievements. Time-related data can also reveal a pattern of change in a community's resource endowment and its utilization over time. In planning and evaluating sustainable development, it is useful to understand significant events in a community's past because they may influence present attitudes and behaviors.

Community timelines and trend lines should be prepared by the local people based on their discussions about and understanding of influential events related to community programs or issues. Group discussions provide opportunities to ask long-term community residents about the community's experiences, challenges, responses, successful strategies, accomplishments, and opportunities.

Social data may be collected by: (1) interviewing members of a household, and (2) analyzing institutions in the community. Household interviews give an Appraisal Team the chance to talk with residents who may not otherwise be included in the Participatory Rural Appraisal process. Normally, a cross section of households is interviewed to gain an understanding of variations among families within the community. The interviews are informal, based on a predeveloped interview schedule (questionnaire), and may cover a variety of topics, which include household and community characteristics, resource management practices, and community problems and opportunities. Interviews about a household should be conducted with appropriate adult head(s) of that household by competent interviewers with appropriate research attitudes.

It is important to identify and clarify activities of various institutions (*institutional analysis*) within the community, to understand the relationships among them and to determine which institutions enjoy the respect and confidence of the community. Institutional analysis involves the use of discussion groups that consist of local residents, community leaders, and other interested parties to determine the role of each institution as it relates to the community.

Technical data (including figures for economic analysis and budgeting) should be collected as soon as (but not before) priority problems and options become clear. For instance, if it becomes evident, at some point during the course of a Participatory Rural Appraisal, that water quality is emerging as a top priority for the community, the interested parties may decide to collect more technical data on water quality. It may them be useful to prepare detailed technical surveys and a financial analysis to enhance the discussion of water at community planning meeting(s). In general, the people should decide when to collect technical data, how much to collect, and how detailed a survey or projected economic analysis will be based on community needs and prevailing circumstances. Finally, the people must analyze and interpret the data in a participatory fashion.

After analyzing the data, community members and other interested parties must get together and discuss the results. Participants will typically rank the identified problems and then rank the perceived opportunities for addressing the most critical or severe of the problems. The best opportunities can then be written into the *community resource management plan*—which describes actions to be taken, who is responsible for each action, resources needed, and the schedule of the implementation plan. The great thing about such a plan is that it is derived, adopted, implemented, and managed by the people themselves for themselves.

Deciding Which Techniques to Use

Although not exhaustive, we have discussed a variety of methods for collecting data, some in greater detail than others. The methods described here are not mutually exclusive. These methods can, therefore, be used either separately or eclectically as a people find suitable for the particular evaluation with which they are faced.

The method(s) used should be selected based on the information the group wants to collect, the research method being used, and what exactly the group wants to measure. Other important factors to be considered before choosing a given method for collecting data are their: (1) ability to use a given method and associated tool(s), (2) ability to get support, if needed, to use the chosen method, (3) ability to pay the cost(s) associated with the method chosen, (4) amount of resources available for the evaluation, and (5) ramifications associated with alternative methods in terms of type, scope, and quality of data that can be obtained.

Clearly, there is no need to use a sophisticated data collection method or tool if a group has a simpler way to achieve the same objectives. Collecting data does not have to be complex or costly. With a little creativity, any group can adapt or develop tools and methods for gathering data that are effective, affordable, and convenient for them.

Not all methods are appropriate for every project at hand. Further, the appropriateness of some methods may not be readily apparent or easily determined, which calls for a systematic and participatory approach to selecting the method of data collection itself. It is thus advisable to first brainstorm the available possibilities for data collection and then consider the appropriateness of each method with respect to the given evaluation before choosing which one(s) to use.

Despite the adaptability of procedures, local residents may be unsure of what options are available or appropriate for collecting data to gain needed information. At such times, they might benefit from help in identifying sources of information and in choosing methods for collecting data. But ultimately, each community or group engaged in evaluation has to determine the following for itself: (1) what questions to ask, (2) which indicators to monitor, (3) which tools to use, (4) who will collect the information, (5) how to collect the information efficiently and effectively, and (6) how to insure that the information collected is accurate, complete, and useful.

To address these six points, the following criteria, recommended by community development practitioner Jim Rugh, are suggested:[23]

- The selected technique should complement the approach and philosophy of the project.

- Community participants should perceive it as a way to help them solve their problems, not just information about them gathered by or for outsiders.

- Those involved in collecting information should understand why it is needed and, as much as possible, be a part of analyzing and using the findings.

- Match techniques used to the skills and aptitudes of the participants.

- The selected technique should allow ample time for normal responsibilities.

- The selected technique should focus on a minimum number of well chosen indicators.

- The selected technique should provide timely information that is actually needed for decision making.

- The results should be statistically reliable and objective enough to convince others of their credibility, even if not quantitative.

- The sophistication and cost of the technique(s) used should be in keeping with the level of evaluation called for—simpler for more routine evaluations, perhaps more complex for an occasional major evaluation.

- Whatever techniques are used, they should reinforce a feeling of community solidarity, cooperation, and involvement.

Further, Rugh reminds us, that the tool used in collecting data influences what is learned from the data. For instance, open-ended interviews may reveal subjective perceptions of people about a given issue, project, or community, while methods that rely on physical evidence may reveal more objective or quantitative aspects of reality that are both different and complementary to the former. Thus a combination of techniques makes findings more valid and reliable by enabling a community to capture a more complete perspective of the phenomenon being evaluated.

Depending on the project and the situation, data collection can take a considerable amount of time. It is therefore important to plan ahead and schedule enough time for each anticipated activity, including analyzing (making sense of) the data collected and learning from it.

4

ANALYZING AND INTERPRETING DATA

In planning and evaluating sustainable development, it is imperative that we use data as a basis for informed conversation and decision making that involves all concerned—not as a means of forcing certain decisions on people or overlooking other alternatives. Thus, collected data should be presented to all interested parties in ways that enhance the quality of their participation. Before we can do this, however, the data have to be analyzed. This entails examining the data first to make sure that it is useful, and then applying appropriate procedures to analyze and interpret the data, which can be qualitative, quantitative, or both.

Examine the Data

The first step in analysis of data is to thoroughly examine the data and unequivocally determine that they are accurate, logical, and suitable. In other words, one needs to make sure there are no obvious signs of potential problems that would lead to questions concerning the quality, integrity, or appropriateness of the data. Signs of problems include data that do not reflect the expected sample size, number of variables, specific variable(s) of interest, given community or geographic area, demographic characteristics, and so on.

Suppose, for instance, one is studying the agricultural practices of organic farmers in community "A," but a preliminary review of the data shows that some respondents are not "organic farmers" or that they live in community "B." Ostensibly, such information would raise a "red" flag and potentially challenge one's faith in the data. The point is to make sure the data are "good" before proceeding with analysis.

By way of example, suppose participants in a community-wide study on solar water heaters were asked to complete surveys with questions such as:

1. Have you used a solar water heater before?

2. What type: Make_____ Model_____?

3. In what ways, if any, did it meet or exceed your expectations?

4. In what ways, if any, did it fall short of your expectations?

If a respondent answered "No" to question number 1, meaning that he or she has never used a solar water heater, then it is only logical that the respondent should choose "not applicable" for questions 2, 3, and 4. Should a respondent who answered "No" to question number 1, go ahead to state the make and model of a solar heater and/or list ways in which the solar water heater met or did not meet his or her expectations, that would be inconsistent with the previous response (to question number 1). This would be a sign of something wrong with the data, including the possibility that the data were entered (transferred) incorrectly or that the respondent gave false or incorrect answer(s). It is therefore essential to identify such inconsistencies early so errors in data entry can be corrected and thus eliminate invalid responses before actual analysis begins. One way to audit data is to determine if the information makes sense.

While the adage "garbage in garbage out" may sound dramatic, it highlights the importance of determining the quality of one's data before going through the motions of analysis and interpretation. Only after one is reasonably sure the data are good is one ready to actually analyze it, using qualitative and/or quantitative methods as appropriate for the given data.

We begin our discussion with qualitative data analysis because it answers the questions of what happens and why it happens. Why something happens is critical to understanding any given relationship as part of an interactive system.

American psychologist Jean Houston tells a wonderful anecdote about the life of anthropologist Margaret Mead.[24] It seems that Margaret, as a child, asked her mother to teach her how to make cheese. "Yes, dear," her mother replied, "but you are going to have to watch the calf being born." Margaret was thus taught as a child to participate in the entire process—from the beginning, through the middle, to the end. This is an important concept because a calf must be born before a brick of cow's cheese can be produced. Why? Because cheese, be it cow or otherwise, is dependent on a baby being born so the mother will have milk with which to nourish it. And it is the same milk that we humans use to make cheese.

Unfortunately, laments Dr. Houston, we are products of an "age of interrupted processes" in which we flip a switch and the world is set into motion as if by magic. We may know a little about the beginning and ending of things, but we are sorely ignorant about the middle of almost everything.

If we all knew what Margaret Mead had learned, we would also know that, every system is defined by the interrelationship of all of its parts as a functional whole and *not* by the sum of its separate parts in isolation of their relationship to one another. Without an understanding of the whole in relationship to the parts and the parts in relationship to the whole, little is understood. Thus, while qualitative data gives us the what and why, quantitative data tells us what happens and the *magnitude* of its happening—in other words, what and *how much*.

Once we understand why something happens, the magnitude of its effect makes sense in terms of understanding a system's dynamics, which is the essence of evaluating the sustainability of anything. The *why* without the magnitude and the *magnitude* without the why is each but half of the equation that leads to understanding the sustainability of any system one chooses to analyze, which bring us to a discussion of qualitative data analysis.*

Analyzing Qualitative Data

As authors Andrea Vierra and Judith Pollock noted, "to analyze data means to examine them critically and to determine their essential characteristics."[25] Qualitative data analysis involves simplification and organization of data into basic units, categories, and patterns in order to determine and summarize their essential characteristics. It is imperative, when analyzing qualitative data, to focus the analysis on the central issues or questions the evaluation is meant to address.

A good way of focusing data analysis is to review the questions generated at the beginning, as well as related discussions and decisions that can help clarify the purpose of the evaluation. Only with a clear and appropriate focus, should one proceed with the main job of analyzing qualitative data, which is to distill the data in a way that not only reduces the volume, but also captures the essential information contained in the data.

One must begin by examining available data to make sure the quality is acceptable and the information complete and sufficient for meeting the needs of the evaluation, such as making sure all necessary field notes or interview transcriptions are intact and in hand. If there is data-related work in progress (for example, film being processed), that must be finished in order to have a complete set of data to analyze. In addition, verification of data in the field through feedback and attention to matters of interpretation is an essential part of quality assurance. Unlike the analysis of quantitative data, where data are typically analyzed after everything has been collected, qualitative data collection and analysis are often interactive; informing and guiding

---

* A group can also start with quantitative analysis of numerical variables in their study. However, it is essential that they understand and report the meaning behind such results, which makes qualitative data analysis imperative.

one another.[26] Thus, there exists no definite line to mark the end of data collection and the beginning of analysis.[27]

Besides making sure that the data being used are appropriate, valid, complete, and focusing the analysis to address the questions, the process of qualitative data analysis involves the following additional steps:

- Organize data to bring some structure and order to the mass of information
- Find themes or topics within the data
- Identify categories emerging from the data
- Search for patterns or relationships among the categories
- Code data to keep track of emerging categories and relationships among them
- Determine findings, such as what was observed or said
- Interpret findings, e.g., the meaning and implication of what happened

Qualitative data are typically collected in a naturalistic fashion, not a predetermined or organized format. In order to extract the essential information from the data, which tends to be extensive, it is advisable to organized the data based on: (1) questions generated during the conceptual and design phase of the project, and (2) analytical insights and interpretations that emerged during data collection.[28]

Further, the data should be examined critically to determine their essential characteristics by identifying distinct categories within the data, as well as looking for emerging patterns of similarities, differences, and relationships within and among those categories. The following story illustrates the above point.

In January 2000, the Board of Directors of the University of Minnesota Northeast Regional Sustainable Development Partnership went through a planning process aimed at determining the board's working goals for the year 2000. To generate ideas (data), individual board members were asked to respond to a question: "What should our work goals for year 2000 be?" The responses for the nine participants are listed in Table 4.1 below (according to the nine participants).

As can be seen from a quick review of Table 4.1, such raw data does not do a good job of helping people answer important questions. To actually answer the question of what the group's work goals should be, the individual responses had to be analyzed to determine what the group was saying, thus moving from individual ideas to the group's judgment,[29] which was done by critically examining individual responses to find relationships and patterns. The analysis was done as follows: First, responses that can be grouped together were identified. Second, the identified categories were appropriately named, for example, subject, or topic. Finally, the results were summarized under four general categories (Table 4.2).

The process of organizing qualitative data involves: (1) looking for *convergence* or how parts of the data fit together in order to identify patterns or distinct categories as described above, and (2) looking for *divergence,* which means comparing the emerging categories to make sure that they are really distinct from one another.[30] In the above example, convergence was sought first and resulted in the data falling into the four general categories (Board Membership and Operation, Communication and Public Involvement, Project Development and Implementation, and Evaluation of our Program and Projects). Following that, divergence among the four categories was investigated by examining items under each of these categories to see if: (1) any item fitted better under another category; (2) there were categories that should be collapsed to eliminate redundancy; and (3) new categories should be created to accommodate additional distinct elements that did not fit nicely into any of the existing categories.

The example cited above is a relatively simple case. Typically, qualitative data analysis involves voluminous data that may include a lot of interview transcripts, field notes, observations,

Table 4.1   Goals Suggested by Individual Participants

- Add to board; progress with projects; develop progression on board; leadership and involvement; more clearly identify concerns; strong communication; go with the sustainability forum suggested by Dan.

- Let public know who we are; work to get full board; try to get some good projects to work on; work with tourism industry sustainability; try to get someone from minerals and mining on board.

- Increase visibility of Northeast Region Sustainable Development Partnership through listening tours and community meetings; increase board membership; create a few high quality, high visibility projects; and establish good working relationship with new extension district director.

- Board member recruitment (diversification) and education; develop and implement a communication plan, i.e., public relations, legislation; identify and prioritize primary issues; develop evaluation plan; develop and maintain an effective project 'process'; asset mapping; environmental scans similar to that conducted by the Experiment in Rural Cooperation in southeastern Minnesota.

- Pare board meetings to essentials: small group discussion, bring issues and/or problems from region; conferences on sustainable development; identify board priorities; clarify our role to region people, assets, goals; food project; fund my projects.

- Add to board; progress with projects; develop progression on board; identify concerns; communication; Dan's forum.

- Fully commit available funding to sustainability projects; communicate purpose and role of partnership to a broad audience in northeast Minnesota; expand and diversify board membership; link more closely with county-based extension educators (source of contacts and ideas); develop and/or fund a regional project related to forest management and/or sustainability.

- Get word out, one goal is to get the word out about who we are and what we do. My ideas include articles in area papers with examples of projects we have currently funded. At the same time,

Continued

Table 4.1 *Continued*

we can advertise for the desire to increase membership. Could end the article with: "For further information, contact Okey Ukaga or board member closest to the area in which the paper is distributed." Add new members, add more board members. Nomination process has to be defined. We can't keep changing nomination process; let's focus on new members, keep our eyes and ears open to potential candidates for board members and interested parties so we can get the word out. Network with extension people or other parties who promote sustainability. Simplify RFP process.

- Increase board size by six representatives; streamline the project application; educate and/or inform board on project list from other areas; update status report on projects.

Table 4.2 Summary and Organization of Goals Suggested by Participants

Board Membership and Operation
- Pare Board meetings to essentials

- Expand and diversify Board membership

- Clarify and stop changing the nomination process

Communication and Public Involvement
- Develop and implement a communication and public involvement plan

- Continue to inform a broad audience in northeast Minnesota about our purpose/work

- Increase visibility of Northeast Region Sustainable Development Partnership through listening tours and community meetings

- Work with communication committee to keep legislators and other stakeholders informed

- Work with the other regions and the Statewide Coordinating Committee to develop a statewide legislative strategy

- Use a variety of methods to get the word out about who we are and what we do

Table 4.2   *Continued*

Project Development and Implementation

- Fully commit available funding to sustainability projects

- Continue to implement current projects

- Identify and develop new projects using a variety of methods

- Simplify the Request for Proposal and/or application process environmental scans across the region to identify and prioritize primary issues

- Involve local people in identifying and clarifying needs, priorities, assets, and goals

- Work with the tourism industry to promote "sustainability"

- Link more closely with county-based extension educators

- Develop and/or fund a regional project related to forest management and/or sustainability

- Finalize the action plan for the community food systems project and start project implementation

- Continue to educate and inform the Board on current projects and list of projects from other areas

Evaluate our Program and Projects

- Continue the annual assessment and program evaluation

- Work with partners to monitor and evaluate funded projects on an ongoing basis

---

photographs, videos, audiotapes, and other private and public documents, which can make categorization complex. It is therefore recommended that some kind of coding be used, especially when dealing with large data, to keep track of emerging categories and to facilitate the organization of the data.

As topics, themes, and categories emerge, *coding* may be used to facilitate tracking and organizing the different components of the data, especially as the analysis gets complex. Participants should use their discretion in deciding when and how to code. But the more complex the categories, patterns, and analysis, the more important it is to use a coding system. Further, it is important for a group to use a coding system that is effective, makes sense to the users, and is easy to apply.

Organizing Data from Within and Without

Qualitative data can be organized from an insider's perspective (called *emic* in research jargon) or from an outside observer's viewpoint (*etic*). To start with, evaluation of sustainable development should employ the participants' ways of thinking or *emic* categories in collecting, organizing, and interpreting data because the goal is to capture and reproduce what is happening from an insider's viewpoint. Nevertheless, an outside observer's perspective or insight can be useful in linking the insiders' view of their community to a more global environment. Andrea Vierra and Judith Pollock describe the different but complementary uses of inside and outside perspectives as follows:

> Although qualitative field research is primarily concerned with insider categories in data collection, outsider explanations are important in data analysis. Outsider categories are employed in the design of the project and in data analysis because the explanations belong to a larger universe than insider categories and, thus, are essential for making a distinctive social setting comprehensible and meaningful to people outside. Insider categories enable researchers to understand how people within an organization perceive their world, whereas outsider categories help researchers explain those perceptions to other people.[31]

The following story illustrates how an outsider's concept or perspective is used to help understand or clarify how a group of insiders define their world. In June of 1999, the Board of Directors of University of Minnesota Northeast Region Sustainable Development Partnership went through a strategic planning process during which they developed a plan of work with the various elements that they organized according to the following categories: (1) vision, (2) desired outcomes, and (3) ideas for action (see Appendix 2). Thus the data were organized using the insider's (emic) categories or how the Sustainable Partnership Board of Directors perceives their world.

The outsider's (etic) perspective came from the work of Drs. Cornelia Flora and Jan Flora (two Iowa State University professors) with the Board of Directors while serving as endowed chairs in agriculture at University of Minnesota. Upon review of the data generated by the Sustainable Development Partnership at the June 1999 planning meeting, professors Jan and Cornelia Flora reorganized the data through their etic framework. Specifically, they classified the outcomes identified by the Sustainable Development Partnership into the following categories:

- Social capital

- Human capital

- Financial capital

- Natural capital

Further, their framework called for linking identified "outcomes" (such as "people will know and want to live sustainably") with specific "outputs" (such as " less waste and consumption") and in turn to specific activities necessary for achieving the desired outcome (such as "join with other organizations to conduct research on sustainable transportation"). The concept points out that it is necessary to have specific activities that lead to the desired outputs that, in turn, lead to the desired outcomes (see Appendix 3).

Examination of the data by all stakeholders using both insiders' and outsiders' perspectives makes the data more meaningful to outsiders but also enlightens insiders and enables them to identify gaps in both their information and process that need to be filled. For instance, going back to the story about the Sustainable Development Partnership, it was discovered, as a result of looking at the data from both the board members and the professors perspectives, that it was necessary to do a better job of identifying and specifying activities and outputs that would lead to the desired outcomes identified by the institutional actors. This would most likely not have happened had the analysis used only the board members' perspective.

As data analysis progresses and the evaluators get more familiar with the data, patterns emerge and increasing attention turns to verification of preliminary findings. Professor Edgar Yoder, of Pennsylvania State University, suggests the following strategies for verification and validation of qualitative data:

1. Look for rival explanations or themes: If rival explanations are not found, the original theme or explanation look more plausible.

2. Search for negative cases: Determine if there are cases that do not fit the emerging hypothesis or trend and examine what they have to offer.

3. Triangulate or compare various types and sources of data: Compare findings from multiple sources of data; compare information across data collectors and interpreters (if any) within the group; compare information collected at different times; and compare the information from the qualitative data with quantitative data.[32]

Analyzing Quantitative Data

A common way to analyze quantitative data is with statistics, which help one to reduce, summarize, and make sense of large amounts of data.* There are a variety of descriptive and inferential statistical procedures that can be used to analyze quantitative data.

---

* Refers to numbers such as a percentage or an average computed to summarize data. "Statistics" also refers to an academic subject area—a branch of mathematics—that deals with analysis of data. The term "statistics" may also be used to refer to raw data such as statistics on agricultural activities in a community.

As their names imply, *descriptive statistics* are used to describe large amounts of data economically and accurately, while *inferential statistics* are used to draw inferences or conclusions about a given population based on a sample(s) from that population.

Descriptive Statistics

Percentages, ratios, proportions, mean, mode and median, range, standard deviation, and variance are all examples of descriptive statistics that evaluators find useful for reducing large quantities of data to a manageable and easily understood form. By way of illustration, consider the following scenario:

One hundred consumers out of the total population in a certain town were asked the following question: "Are you in favor of or against labeling food produced with genetically modified organisms?" Some said they were against labeling, while others said they were in favor of it. The responses can be listed as follows:

Respondent	Answer	Respondent	Answer
1	Favor	17	Against
2	Against	18	Favor
3	Favor	19	Favor
4	Favor	20	Against
5	Against	21	Favor
6	Against	22	Favor
7	Favor	23	Against
8	Favor	24	Favor
9	Favor	25	Favor
10	Against	26	Against
11	Favor	27	Against
12	Against	28	Favor
13	Favor	29	Against
14	Against	30	Favor
15	Favor	31	Against
16	Favor	32	Favor

Respondent	Answer	Respondent	Answer
33	Favor	67	Against
34	Against	68	Favor
35	Favor	69	Against
36	Favor	70	Favor
37	Against	71	Against
38	Favor	72	Favor
39	Favor	73	Favor
40	Against	74	Against
41	Favor	75	Favor
42	Favor	76	Favor
43	Against	77	Against
44	Favor	78	Favor
45	Favor	79	Favor
46	Against	80	Favor
47	Favor	81	Against
48	Favor	82	Favor
49	Favor	83	Favor
50	Against	84	Against
51	Favor	85	Favor
52	Against	86	Favor
53	Favor	87	Against
54	Against	88	Favor
55	Favor	89	Against
56	Against	90	Favor
57	Favor	91	Favor
58	Favor	92	Against
59	Against	93	Favor
60	Favor	94	Against
61	Favor	95	Favor
62	Against	96	Against
63	Favor	97	Against
64	Favor	98	Favor
65	Against	99	Against
66	Favor	100	Against

This approach, as you can see, is not only inefficient but also ineffective in helping people comprehend the data because the human mind tends to have difficulty with both comprehending and remembering large quantities of data unless distilled and presented in manageable, succinct, and crisp fashion. So data need to be simplified and reduced in order to be presented in an intelligible manner.

Basic descriptive statistics, such as frequencies, ratios, proportions, and percentages, can be used to reduce and simplify the above data as follows:

First, the data can be simplified by dividing the respondents into two groups (that is, those that favor labeling; those opposed) and presenting the frequencies (which is number of occurrences) associated with each group. In this case, the frequency associated with "yes, label" is 60 and the frequency of "no label" is 40. Second, proportions can be used to report that 6/10 consumers surveyed were in favor of labeling and that 4/10 were against it. Third, one can use ratios to express the number of those who are in favor of labeling in relation to those who are not. In this case, the ratio of those who favor labeling to those who are not is 6:4. And fourth, percentages can be used to analyze the above data, which will show that 40 percent of the respondents are against labeling food produced with genetically modified organisms while 60 percent are in favor of labeling. Further, graphs such as pie chart (Figure 4.1) and bar/column graph (Figure 4.2) can be used to illustrate and present the data more effectively.

Figure 4.1   Pie Chart Showing Percent of People in Favor and Against Labelling

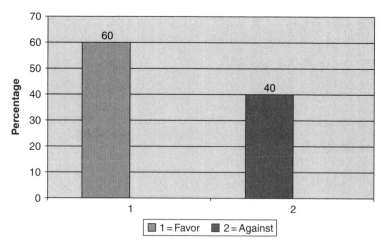

Figure 4.2 Column Chart Showing Percent of People in Favor/Against Labelling

Now let's look at another example. Suppose one asks 200 respondents how many siblings they each have. And suppose 14 respondents said they have 0 siblings, 40 said 2 siblings, 66 said 3 siblings, 42 said 4 siblings, 16 said 5 siblings, 8 said 6 siblings, 6 said 7 siblings, 4 said 8 siblings, 2 said 9 siblings, and 2 reported 10 siblings. Although the answers of the 200 individual responses can be listed, such a long list would be both inefficient and ineffective, as in the previous example. Again, one is better off using frequencies, percentages, ratios, and proportions to analyze the data and communicate the findings. One can, for instance, summarize the data by presenting the percentages or frequencies associated with 0, 2, 3, 4, 5, 6, 7, 8, 9, and 10 siblings (Table 4.3).

The data can also be presented in terms of proportions or ratios of various numbers of siblings in relation to other(s) if one is interested in comparing two or more categories; or even more effectively with graphs such as we saw in the previous example.

Let's continue our review of basic descriptive statistics by considering yet another example. Suppose the weight (in

Table 4.3   Number of Siblings Reported
by Respondents (Ungrouped Data)

Number of Siblings	Frequency	Percentage
Zero	14	7
Two	40	20
Three	66	33
Four	42	21
Five	16	8
Six	8	4
Seven	6	3
Eight	4	2
Nine	2	1
Ten	2	1
Total	200	100%

pounds) of 100 adults was sampled from a certain population. Which statistics would be most useful in this case?

To begin with, it is important to note that, unlike the previous example, where the variable (number of siblings) is discrete, the variable in this case (weight in pounds) is continuous—meaning that an individual's weight could be 170.123 lbs, 170.5 lbs, 162.17 lbs, 203 lbs, and so on. Thus, unlike the previous example, where it was found that 7, 20, 33, 21, 8, 4, 3, and 2 respondents had 0, 1, 2, 3, 4, 5, 6, 7, and 8 siblings respectively, the chances of observing individuals in this sample with exactly the same weight are limited. In fact, one may never observe more than one individual that weighs 170.123 lbs, or 170.5 lbs, or 162.17 lbs, or 203.1 in the sample.

Therefore, data on continuous variable (respondent's weights in this case) is best grouped into classes or cells from which to calculate the statistics, such as frequency or percentage for each class. This is because it is generally both inefficient and ineffective to talk about the percentage or frequency of a specific value of *continuous variables* like weight, height, age, and so on, since the chances of having subjects with exactly the same value are limited. Instead, we can group the subjects into a few classes within the range of data, and then calculate the needed statistics for each cell.

Suppose, for instance, that we have data on the weight of the 100 people that range from 70 lbs to 230 lbs. Rather than report the frequency or percentage associated with each and every weight observed, we may group the subjects into 8 cells, for instance, and report the frequency as follows (Table 4.4).

There is no hard rule for determining the number of cells. It can be done arbitrarily as long as the cells: (a) strike a reasonable balance between too much detail and too little, and (b) result in a convenient whole-number midpoint in each class because the midpoint will represent all sample values in that class.[33]

Now suppose one prefers to use a single statistic to describe how a sample frequency is distributed. For instance, the most

Table 4.4   Frequency of the Weight of a Sample of 100 People (Grouped Data)

Cell	Class	Frequency
1.	70–90 lbs	1
2.	90–110 lbs	5
3.	110–130 lbs	12
4.	130–140 lbs	20
5.	150–170 lbs	29
6.	170–190 lbs	27
7.	190–210 lbs	7
8.	210–230 lbs	3

important piece of information that people may want to extract from and share about the data referred to above may be the typical weight of the people studied. In other words, how heavy or light are the people in general?

Frequencies, percentages, ratios, and proportion cannot answer the above question with a single statistic. Thus, the descriptive statistics that we have discussed so far in this chapter do not do a great job of giving a general view of the data.

To glean a good general view of the data, two kinds of descriptive statistics, commonly known as *measures of central tendencies* and *measures of dispersion,* are needed. In other words, a single central tendency statistic (such as the mean, the median, and the mode), are necessary to glean an indication of the center of a frequency distribution and a dispersion or variability statistic (such as the range, the standard deviation, and variance), tells how the data is dispersed (spread). These are summarized in Table 4.5 according to what they measure and the type of data (that is, nominal, ordinal, interval/ratio) for which they are appropriate.

Nominal variables, such as gender, are classified into categories, like male and female. Ordinal variables, such as student classification or faculty rank, are also classified into categories, but as the name implies, the categories (for example, freshman, junior, and senior or assistant, associate, and full professor) have some order. Interval variables and ratio variables, such as height, age, and income generally have equal distances between two points on the scale of measurement. For instance, the distance from one foot to two feet as a measure of distance is the same as from two feet to three feet as a measure of distance, which is the same as from three to four, and so on. Examples of interval scale variables include such things as age measured in years, height measured in feet, and weight measured in pounds. Examples of variables measured in ratio scale include income measured in dollars per year and speed measured in miles per hour.

Table 4.5 Summary of Selected Descriptive Statistics for Use with Various Scales

	Type of Data		
Type of Measure	Nominal	Ordinal	Interval/Ratio
Central Tendency	Mode	Median	Mean, Median
Spread/Variability	Frequency	Median, Range	Variance, Standard Deviation, Range
Symmetry	Not Applicable	Not Applicable	Data distribution can be negatively skewed (to the left), or symmetrical, or positively skewed (to the right)
Kurtosis	Not Applicable	Not Applicable	The distribution can have a peaked curve (leptokurtic), or normal curve (mesokurtic), or flat (platykurtic)

The Mean

The arithmetic *mean* or simple average is the most commonly used measure of central tendency. It is derived by dividing the sum of all observations by the number of observations. In other words, it is calculated by adding the figures (in this case weights of the respondents) and dividing the total by the number of items (in this case 100). If every one in the sample weighed 170 lbs, the total weight would be 170 times 100 which is 17,000, and the mean or average weight would be 170. Thus, the mean is very useful in figuring and discussing variables that are measured in interval/ratio scales, such as the average daily consumption of water per person or per household, the mean annual temperature of a city or Bioregion, and so on.

In addition to being a useful descriptive tool familiar to many people, the mean takes the entire data set into account because it is algebraically based. Nevertheless, the mean—like other statistics—has limitations. Notably, it is influenced by extreme values and may not be a true representative of a data set with a skewed distribution.

For instance, suppose we study the income of 10 families in a certain community and find the annual income of families 1 through 10 to be $22,990, $33,000, $36,000, $40,000, $45,000, $48,900, $50,000, $59,000, $60,000, and $1,000,000. It will be misleading to report the average income of these families to be $139,489, which is what we would get if we calculate the mean of the above data set. The problem is that the $1,000,000 income of family number 10, which is an extreme figure, has influenced the mean and caused it to give a view of the other nine families that is unrealistic. Another limitation of the mean is that it cannot be calculated from an open-ended distribution, meaning one that has no lower or upper limit.

The Mode

The *mode* is the simplest measure of central tendency. It is defined as the value in the data set that has the highest frequency of occurrence. In other words, it is the most frequent value. In our example dealing with siblings, the mode is 3. More people (33) had three siblings than any other number of siblings. It is pertinent to note that, depending on the data, the mode can be more than one. Consider, for instance, that of the 100 people surveyed, 40 have 2 siblings and 40 have 3 siblings, while the remaining 20 have various numbers of siblings. In the above example, both 2 siblings and 3 siblings have the highest frequency or occurrence (40). Hence, we have two modes (2 and 3) in this example.

When there are two or more modes, the meaning may be ambiguous and caution must be exercised when using mode in such cases. Further, the mode often depends not only on how data are grouped but also can be shifted by changing how data are grouped, which greatly impinges on its reliability.

The Median

The *median* is the observation or value that is found at the center of a data set when observations or values are arranged in an ascending or descending order. For this reason, the median is also called the middle value or the 50th percentile. In a sample with an odd total number of observations, the median can easily be identified by arranging the data in an ascending or descending order and selecting the observation in the middle, which is the value above and below which 50 percent of the observations fall.

When, however, the total number of observations is an even number, the median is not readily apparent. In this case, the median would be the *average* of the two middle values. To determine the median in such a case, one would first arrange the data in descending or ascending order, then identify the two values in the middle, and finally, calculate the average of the two values.*

Although people may be most interested in a value that represents the group, such as the average body weight of those people studied, it is equally important to have some indication of how that weight is distributed within the group. To do this, one uses some other kinds of descriptive statistics to measure the spread (dispersion).

Dispersion

Dispersion, or the spread of values within a particular set of data can be measured by using *range, standard deviation,* and *variance.* Let's begin with range, which is the distance between the largest value and the smallest value in a data set. Range is

---

* The two procedures suggested above assume of course that we have ungrouped data. But where we have grouped data, we can calculate the median value by choosing a value within the median cell that corresponds approximately with the middle (50th percentile).

the simplest measure of dispersion. It can be calculated by sub-
tracting the smallest value in the data set from the largest value.
A major limitation of range as a measure of spread is that it does
not tell much about the distribution of the data except where it
starts and where it ends (the largest and smallest scores), and as
we found with the income of the ten families discussed earlier,
the largest and smallest scores are not necessarily reliable indicators of how the data are distributed.

For example, consider the annual income of the 10 families
discussed above. The first nine families earned $22,990,
$33,000, $36,000, $40,000, $45,000, $48,900, $50,000,
$59,000, and $60,000 respectively, while family number 10
earned $1,000,000. The range for this data is $977,010.00
($1,000,000 minus $22,990.00). Obviously, this is not a fair
representation of how the income is distributed among the first
nine families, which underscores the limitation of using range as
a measure of spread because it considers only the extreme values. To more effectively measure the spread of such data, one
needs a measure that takes into account all observations within
the data set.

Variance is one measure of dispersion that accounts for all
observations within a data set. It is derived by: (1) determining the
mean of all scores in the data set, (2) calculating the difference
between each score and the mean of scores to get deviation scores
for each observation, (3) squaring each of these deviation scores,
(4) adding all the squared mean deviations, and (5) dividing the
total mean deviation by the number of observations to get average
mean deviation. Thus, variance is the average of the squares of
the deviation of the scores from the mean. However, we almost
never use it as a descriptive statistic, but in the calculation of
other more commonly used statistics like the standard deviation.

Standard deviation is the most common measure of spread. It
is another measure of dispersion that takes into account all components of a data set. Standard deviation is the square root of
variance. Look at step number four above and note that we

squared each of the deviation scores in deriving variance. So "by taking the square root [of variance], we compensate for having squared terms in defining variance" and as a result, the standard deviation is reduced to the same units of measurements as the raw data.[34]

In most cases, one or two of the descriptive statistics described above would be all a group needs to summarize available data and communicate it effectively. In such cases, the group should select and use the ones most appropriate for their given evaluation based, among other things, on what they need to measure (for example, spread or central tendency), the type of variable they are dealing with (for example, nominal, ordinal or interval/ratio data). Most importantly, the group must choose the descriptive statistics they can use easily and appropriately given their particular circumstance, such as their available human and material resources. Further, it is always advisable whenever we report a measure of central tendency such as the mean, to also report the corresponding measure of spread like the standard deviation. This is because it is most informative to describe the data in this way (that is, using the mean together with the standard deviation).

Sometimes, however, people are not interested in simply summarizing available data or describing a given phenomenon (which can be done with just *descriptive statistics*). Instead, they may be interested in examining relationships or differences within and/or among the particular population, or they may be interested in drawing inferences about a population based on a sample from the population. Such conclusions require *inferential statistics*.

Inferential Statistics

Inferential statistics are useful for establishing relationships as well as for estimating the parameters of a population with a certain degree of confidence when one does not have information from every member of the population. Some of the more commonly used inferential statistical procedures are summarized

Table 4.6   Examples of Inferential Statistics Used with Various Kinds of Data

Type of Independent Variable	Type of Dependent Variable		
	Nominal	Ordinal	Interval/Ratio
Nominal	Chi Square	Chi Square	T-test Analysis of Variance
Ordinal	Correlation	Correlation	Correlation
	(Rank biserial)	(Spearman rank correlation coefficient)	(Convert interval/ratio data to ordered categories and calculate rank correlation coefficient)
Interval/Ratio	Correlation	Correlation	Regression Correlation
	(Point biserial)	(Convert interval/ratio data to ordered categories and calculate rank correlation coefficient)	(Pearson's product moment correlation coefficient)

below according to the type of data and variable for which they are appropriate (Table 4.6).[35]

Student's t-Test

A t-Test* can be used to test the statistical significance of the difference between means in order to determine if two categories of nominal scale independent variables differ significantly with regard to a given variable that is measured with an interval/ratio

---

* Roger Porkess, *The HarperCollins Dictionary of Statistics* (New York: HarperCollins Publishers, Inc, 1991).

scale. There are generally three kinds of t-Test (*one sample test, two independent sample test,* and *paired sample test*).

One Sample t-Test is used to estimate a population mean using a sample mean. For instance, it was hypothesized that the average amount of water used by Maryville residents is 15 gallons per day; that is, the hypothesis is that each person in Maryville actually uses 15 gallons of water per day. But when the data were collected from a sample of Maryville residents, the average amount of water they actually use (sample mean) turned out to be 16 gallons per day. To determine if there is a statistically significant difference between (a) water use in the sample and (b) the water the population was hypothesized to use, a one sample t-Test is employed.

Two Independent Sample t-Test is used to determine if there is a statistical difference between two independent sample means. Suppose one wants to determine if there is a relationship between gender and income of Maryville residents. In other words, is there a statistical difference between males and females with regard to income? To answer that question, one needs to determine whether (or not) either gender (male or female) is earning significantly more income than the other? Assuming that we have data on income earned by males and females in the given community, we can use *t-Test for two independent means* to determine if there is any difference. Note that, in this case, two independent groups are being compared—one of males, the other of females.

Paired Sample t-Test is used to test for differences between related or paired samples, such as when the scores or values whose means are to be compared case for case are from the same subject. For instance, six Maryville residents participated in a program designed to reduce water consumption by fixing leaks, using low-flow showers, taking five-minute showers, and so on. In order to tell if the program worked, one must compare, and thus determine the amount of water used by this group of people before the water-conservation program was initiated (pre-test) and after (post-test), which requires using the t-Test for paired sample.

A t-Test is used to estimate the difference between two categories of a nominal variable (such as male and female for gender) with regard to scores or values on an interval or ratio scale (such as income, age, height, and so on). But it cannot be used for more than two levels. If, therefore, one wants to determine the difference among three or more levels of nominal independent variables (such as urban, suburban, and rural residence) with regard to scores or values on an interval or ratio scale (such as income, age, height, and so on), one must use a technique called *Analysis of Variance.*

Analysis of Variance

Analysis of Variance is a technique that is used to determine how much variability in a set of observations can be attributed to different causes. It involves separating the sample variance into two components (the variance within the samples and that between or among the samples).

Suppose, for example, that a community is pilot testing three kinds of low-flow showerheads. Now suppose that after measuring the rate of water flow for each type six times, the results, listed in Table 4.7, are obtained. Do these figures support the hypothesis that a significant difference exists among the three types of showers with respect to rate of water flow? A *One-Factor Analysis of Variance (One-Way Analysis of Variance)* can be used to answer the above question since one is dealing with only one factor (that is, type of showerhead).*

---

* This would involve: (1) measuring the rate of water flow in gallons per second for a sample of these showerheads, (2) using the sum of squares* result to separate the variance into two (that within the samples and that between the samples, and (3) using F-Test* to compare these to determine if the variability in data is all random, or if part of it is the result of systematic differences between the samples. If, using the F statistics, we find that the three means are statistically equal, we can conclude that there is no significant difference among the three kinds of showerheads with regard to rate water flows through them. But if, on the other hand differences do exist, go a step further, using the Scheffee Test,* to determine which one has a significantly greater rate of water flow. *See "Introduction to the Practice of Statistics" by Moore and McCabe for more information and guidance on these and other statistical procedures.

Table 4.7   Water Flow Rates of Three Types of Showerheads Measured

Showerheads	Flow rate for each type of showerhead						Mean
Type 1	3.4	3.5	3.6	3.4	3.7	3.5	3.52
Type 2	4.4	4.5	4.3	4.5	4.6	4.3	4.43
Type 3	4.6	4.5	4.7	4.4	4.4	4.5	4.55

Table 4.8   Average Flow Rate of Three Types of Showerheads by Two Sources of Water

Showerheads	Source of Water Supply		Row Mean
	City	Private Well	
Type 1	3.53	3.51	3.52
Type 2	4.30	4.30	4.43
Type 3	4.60	4.50	4.55
Column Mean	4.14	4.10	

But what if one was interested in two factors? Suppose, for example, that in addition to collecting data on rate of water flow by type of showerheads, one also has data on rate of flow by source of water supply, as illustrated in Table 4.8. In this case, one is no longer interested solely in one factor (type of shower) because the source of water supply adds a second factor. Therefore, one needs to use a *Two-Factor Analysis of Variance* also called a *Two-Way Analysis of Variance*. The Two-Way Analysis of Variance employs the same method used in a One-Way Analysis of Variance, but the analysis is extended to determine variations for two factors.

A *Two Factor Analysis of Variance* enables us to determine if the relationship between one independent variable and a dependent variable is different, depending on the category or value of another independent variable. In other words, it would

Table 4.9 Contingency Table Showing Happiness by Gender

Happiness	Gender		
	Male	Female	
Not Happy	30 (50%)	50 (50%)	80
Happy	30 (50%)	50 (50%)	80
	60 (100%)	100 (100%)	160

not only determine the difference among the three types of showers with regard to rate of water flow but also determine if the difference in rate of water flow is affected by another factor, such as the source of water to the shower.

Chi-Square

The Chi-Square test is used (with measures that classify cases into categories, such as male and female) to determine how well observed data fit an expected or theoretical distribution.* It is very useful when one wants to determine if various categories of a nominal independent variable (such as male and female for the variable of gender) differ with regard to categories of some other nominal dependent variable (such as happy and unhappy for the variable of happiness).

Let us suppose, for example, that we want to know if males and females are equally happy about a proposed community project or if they differ in their happiness with respect to the proposed project. In other words, is there a relationship between gender and happiness about the proposed project? To answer this question, one can cross-tabulate the data in such a way that the distribution of values for the dependent variable is subdivided according to the various levels of the independent variable, as in Table 4.9. Then, one can examine the table to see if there

---

* Roger Porkess, *The HarperCollins Dictionary of Statistics* (New York: HarperCollins Publishers, Inc, 1991).

is, in fact, a relationship between the two variables (happiness and gender). In other words, are the numbers and percentages within the cells what you would expect them to be if there were no relationship between gender and happiness? What would you expect to see if gender and happiness are not related?

The previous table shows that 50 percent of the females and 50 percent of the males are happy about the proposed project, while 50 percent of both groups are unhappy. This is what one would expect to see if happiness was not related to gender. Therefore, one can conclude that there is no difference between males and females with regard to their happiness about this project.

But if one observes some difference, as in Table 4.10, one may need to determine whether this difference between male and female with regard to happiness (relationship between gender and happiness) is statistically significant. To find out, Chi-Square is used to test the hypothesis that a relationship exists between gender and happiness.

The Chi-Square test involves comparing the *observed distributions* with the expected distributions (that is, what would be expected if there were no relationship between the two sets of categories). In this case, it would compare the frequency of males and females who are happy and those who are not to see if the differences are within the expected frequency for each category and, if not, to see whether the observed frequency differs enough from that which is expected to be significant. Thus, Chi-Square

Table 4.10   Contingency Table Showing Happiness by Gender

Happiness	Gender		
	Male	Female	
Not Happy	45 (45%)	55 (55%)	85
Happy	30 (50%)	50 (50%)	75
	60 (100%)	100 (100%)	160

is used to determine whether a statistically significant relationship exists between or among two or more nominal variables.* The test shows whether the observed distribution differs sufficiently enough from the expected distribution to be unlikely to have occurred by random sampling, meaning for instance that there is in fact a difference in the population between males and females with regard to happiness.

Correlation Analysis

Correlation Analysis is typically used for the following purposes: (1) to determine the relationship between variables and (2) to predict the value of one variable based on the other. In studying relationship, one correlates the dependent variable with each independent variable to get one correlation coefficient for the relationship between each independent variable and the dependent variable. The correlation of two variables yields a correlation coefficient, a decimal number, between 0.00 and +1.00, or 0.00 and −1.00, which indicates the degree to which those two variables are related. A coefficient near +1.00 means that an increase in one variable is associated with an increase in the other variable and vice versa. If the coefficient is near −1.00, this means that an increase in one variable is associated with a decrease in the other variable and vice versa. While a coefficient of 0.00 means that the variables are not related.[36]

Thus, correlation analysis allows one to determine: (1) if variable X has a direct (positive) relationship with variable Y, which means that as X increases Y increases (see Figure 4.3); or (2) if variable X has an inverse (negative) relationship with variable Y,

---

* When we find a relationship, we may want to determine its strength (i.e. the point where it falls on a continuum between no relationship and a perfect relationship). We can use **Phi Coefficient** to express the strength of the relationship between two variables. It ranges from 0 to 1, where 0 represents no relationship and 1 represents a perfect relationship. But Phi Coefficient would not work for contingency tables that have more than two rows and more than two columns. In such a case, **Cramers V**, a generalized form of Phi Coefficient that takes into account the size of the contingency table, is used instead.

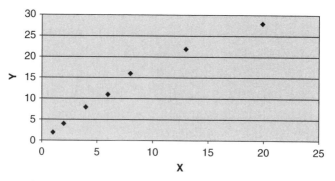

Figure 4.3 Showing Direct (Positive) Relationship between X and Y

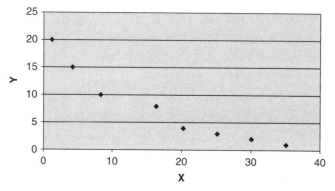

Figure 4.4 Showing Inverse Relationship between X and Y

which means that as X increases, Y decreases (see Figure 4.4), or (3) if variable X has no (zero) relationship with variable Y, which means one cannot predict or explain the value of Y based on X (see Figure 4.5).*

If two variables are associated (correlated) with each other one variable can be predicted with the other. For instance,

---

* Once we find that the variables we are examining are correlated, we may want to also determine the strength of the relationship. This is done by looking at *the coefficient of determination* (r^2) which tells us the proportion of the variation in the dependent variable that is explained by the independent variable. Coefficient of determination ranges from zero to one, where one represents 100 percent correlation (meaning that 100 percent of the variation in the one variable can be explained by a change in the other).

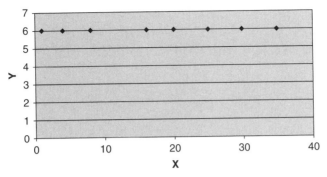

Figure 4.5 Showing No Relationship between X and Y

because the amount of carbon dioxide produced by a certain 20 mile per gallon car is associated with the number of miles it is driven, one can predict how many pounds of carbon dioxide such a car would produce if driven a given number of miles. Data analysis in prediction studies involves correlation of each predictor or independent variable (for example, the number of miles a car is driven) with the criterion or dependent variable (for example, the amount of carbon dioxide produced by the car).

Regression Analysis

Regression analysis can be used to predict or explain a (dependent) variable based on one or more (independent) variable(s). When one variable is used to predict another variable it is called *simple regression*. Simple regression is used when we want to predict x with y or vice versa. The variable we are trying to predict is called a dependent or criterion variable, while the variable that might predict the outcome is called a predictor or an independent variable. Let's suppose we want to predict y with x. By regressing x variable on y, using simple regression analysis, we get an equation that takes the form of $y = a + b x$, where a is the estimated value of y when x is zero, and b indicates expected change in y associated with one unit change in x. This allows us to predict y with x. Additionally, the analysis provides other important information like the coefficient of determination (r^2) that tells how good the regression equation is in predicting the dependent variable y with the independent variable x.

Obviously, we do not expect only one thing in the world to explain or predict all the variation in one variable. Therefore, we may use a combination of variables, instead of only one, to get a more accurate prediction. The predication of a dependent (criterion) variable using a linear combination of two or more independent (predictor) variables is called *multiple regression*. With two variables, for example, the multiple regression equation takes the form of $y = a + b_1(x_1)\ b_2(x_2)$, where a is the estimated value of y when all the independent variables equal zero, while b_1 and b_2 (partial regression coefficients) indicate expected change in y associated with one unit change in x_1 and x_2 respectively. The r^2 (coefficient of determination) in multiple regression tells us how good the regression equation is in predicting the dependent variable y by the linear combination of the independent variables (x_1 and x_2 in this case).

Choosing Statistical Procedures

We have reviewed some of the more common statistical procedures in the preceding sections. There are, nevertheless, other procedures. Any group involved in the evaluation of sustainable development needs to choose statistical procedures that are appropriate for their specific project. Questions to be answered in selecting a statistical technique include:

1. Are the data collected from a random sample or by other means such as a census or non-random sampling?

2. What is the purpose of the evaluation (description or inference)?

3. What is the scale of measurement for dependent variables?

4. How many categories or levels of independent variables do you have?

5. Do you meet the statistical assumptions for the test you plan to use?

If your data are not from a random sample, your options for statistical data analysis are generally limited to descriptive statistics. On the other hand, with data from a random sample, your options would expand to include inferential statistics (see Figure 4.6). Thus, data source not only affects choice of statistical technique, but should as much as possible be determined by the purpose of the evaluation.

To describe a phenomenon, descriptive statistics would be the appropriate choice. However, you still need to select the right descriptive statistics based on exactly what you want to describe and the scale of measurement for the data you have (see Figure 4.7). For example, the mode and frequency distribution are used to *describe* the center and variability respectively, when dealing with nominal scale data; the median and range are used for ordinal data while the mean and standard deviation are used for interval/ratio data.

If on the other hand your purpose were to draw inferences about a population (for example, estimate parameters of a population, or investigate relationships between variables or determine

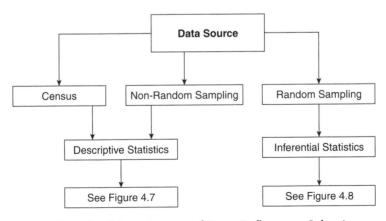

Figure 4.6 Showing How Source of Data Influences Selection of Statistics

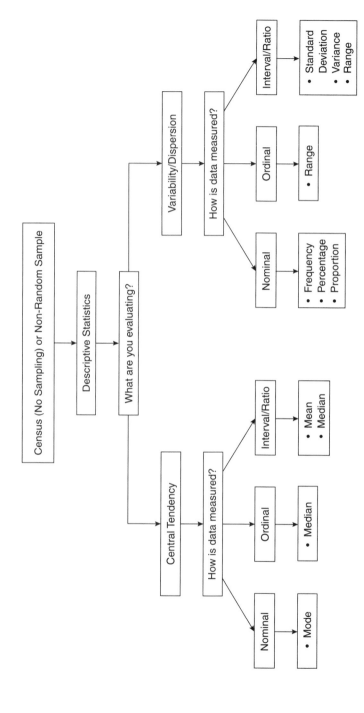

Figure 4.7 Showing Questions and Decisions Involved in Choosing Some Commonly Used Descriptive Statistics

differences between groups) inferential statistics would be an appropriate choice. Again, you still need to select the right inferential statistics based on exactly what you want to evaluate and the scale of data (see Figure 4.8). To estimate *population parameters* based on a random sample, frequency distribution, proportion, and median are used for nominal and ordinal data; mean, proportion, variance and one sample t-Test are used for interval/ratio data. To investigate *relationships,* cross tabulation and Chi-Square are used for nominal data; correlation is used for ordinal, while correlation and regression are used for interval/ratio data. To determine *differences* between/among groups, Chi-Square is used for nominal data; Chi-Square, Analysis of Variance, and correlation is used for ordinal, while t-Test and Analysis of Variance are used for interval/ratio data.

If this is at all confusing, as it may well be to some people who are not familiar with statistical data analysis, it is advisable to seek help in choosing the right statistical procedures and in understanding how to use them appropriately. Assistance can come from more experienced individuals or groups within and outside one's community. Potential sources of professional help include educational institutions, as well as some public, private, and voluntary organizations.

Further, it is pertinent to note that there are a variety of software packages that allows one to generate these statistics, without having to do the complex calculation by hand or even know the computational details involved. Statistical Analysis System (SAS), Statistical Packages for Social Sciences (SPSS), Minitab, and Microsoft Excel are a few examples. Additionally, one can find that basic statistics, which most groups can easily generate, are often sufficient for analyzing and communicating needed information.

Finally, the people should complete the data analysis by deciding, as a group, what the information resulting from the analysis of data really means. Such interpretation of data involves looking at the "big picture." It goes beyond focusing

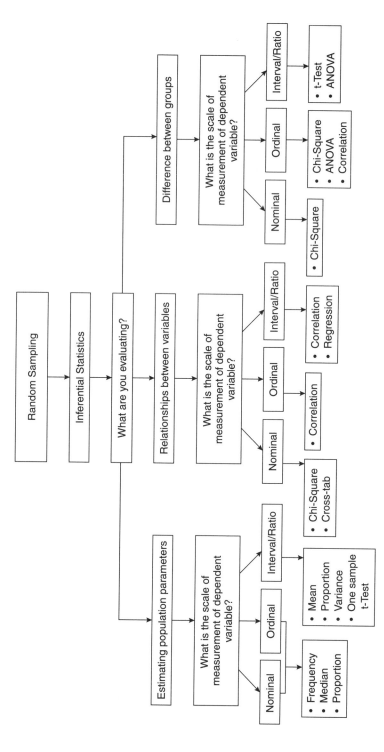

Figure 4.8 Showing Questions and Decisions Involved in Choosing Some Commonly Used Inferential Statistics

narrowly on a specific finding (that is, what was observed) to question whether the finding seems reasonable, to determine the importance of the finding, and what it means or why it happened, and what should be done about it, as we shall discuss in more detail in the next section of this chapter.

Interpreting Findings

To properly interpret data, one has to be able to see the forest (what data mean collectively and how they fit into a more global context) as well as the trees (a specific finding). Interpreting the data in a larger context (the forest) requires one to back up far enough to avoid "tunnel vision," which is essentially concentrating too narrowly on a particular component of the data set (the trees), which is then in danger of being taken out of context of the whole. Proper interpretation of data also requires appreciation and utilization of *other ways of knowing* because a conventional way of seeing things can sometimes be ineffective or inappropriate for the task or question at hand. The following story about two six-year-old children and a mathematics question illustrates the above point.

To assess her students' progress in learning how to do subtraction, a teacher asked the following question: "If there are five birds perching in a tree and somebody shoots down one bird, how many birds are left in the tree?" The first six-year-old said "four," and the second six-year-old said "none." When asked to explain their answers, the first student said if you shoot one out of five, four would be left; in other words, five minus one equals four. Obviously, this was the mathematically correct answer. The second student argued, however, that if one of the five birds were shot out of the tree, all the remaining birds would fly away out of fear of being shot; therefore, none would be left there on the tree. While everyone appreciated and agreed with the logic and wisdom of this six-year-old girl, had she focused only on mathematics with the expected tunnel vision and not applied lateral thinking or another way of seeing things, she would not have given this more realistic answer.

A piecemeal view of things can be concealing at best and misleading at worst. In his book *The Ecology of Commerce,* author Paul Hawken discussed the following story (originally reported in 1992 by the New York Times in an article titled "The Silence of the Frogs"), which illustrates the above point. "At an international conference on herpetology (the study of amphibians and reptiles), while 1,300 participants gave hundreds of official papers on specialized subjects, none had focused on the total picture. Pieced together informally in the hallways and in the lunch lines at the conference was the fact that frogs are disappearing from the face of the earth at an inexplicably rapid rate."[37]

If findings are to be relevant, meaningful, accepted, and used, active involvement of all interested citizens and a sense of total participation is imperative, which means data must be analyzed and interpreted collectively by everyone involved in the project. In fact, we believe that the most important part of evaluating sustainable development is for citizens to collectively participate in the entire evaluation process; it is not the mechanics of crunching numbers and summarizing data.

We therefore encourage every group involved in evaluating sustainable development to be inclusive—rather than exclusive— with respect to analyzing and interpreting data from a common project. We say this because it too often happens that a group either asks those individuals among them who they believe know how to analyze and interpret the data to do so and report the results to the group, *or* they bring in someone from outside to do the analysis and interpretation for them because they think the outsider "knows" what to do and how to do it. In the best cases, however, the group is actively involved in all aspects of the project, as was the case with the following evaluation designed to enable the Sustainable Farming Association of Northeast Minnesota to do strategic planning.

The Sustainable Farming Association

Producers, seeking to establish a tighter network of the ever-dwindling number of farmers in the area and simultaneously help farmers make a transition to more environmentally sound and economically profitable methods of production, formed the Sustainable Farming Association in 1991. The organization has since then played a significant role in supporting local agriculture by working to secure a healthy supply of food, a diversified economy, and thriving rural communities. It also facilitates mutual support and fellowship to strengthen families and communities.

At one point, however, members began to sense that the Sustainable Farming Association had become an organization in transition because managing priorities and deciding the long-term direction of the chapter became challenging. At the same time, members sensed a great potential for their work and the difference they could make for Minnesota in general and their region in particular. The members therefore decided that a comprehensive, strategic plan would help the organization focus its role into the future.

Realizing that they did not have enough funds to create such a strategic plan, the Association sought and got support from the University of Minnesota's Northeast Region Sustainable Development Partnership and other partners (such as the Minnesota Institute for Sustainable Agriculture, the Land Stewardship project, the University of Minnesota Extension Service, local citizens, and communities in Northeast Minnesota) to implement the project. The strategic planning included:

- An initial meeting of the Sustainable Farming Association members, partners, and other interested citizens to plan the evaluation

- A review of lists of names by participants to assure that all interested citizens are actively involved in the project planning and implementation

- The gathering of primary data through surveys, interviews, and focus groups conducted by members of the Association

- A one-day "visioning" meeting during which participants analyzed their data, summarized findings, and started a conversation about what the findings meant with respect to a new vision for the Association

- Another meeting of interested citizens to complete the interpretation of the data and discuss the implications of the findings for the Association

Throughout these activities, the participants were in charge and collectively planned the project and collected, analyzed, and interpreted the data in a manner that was both inclusive and participatory. Although they hired an outside consultant as a facilitator, they used her services appropriately. They did not wait for her to collect, analyze, and interpret the data and then simply hand them a final report. Rather, they let the facilitator "stay in the wings" and guide the process as necessary with a "light touch" while the participants themselves played the central roles and did most of the work. As a result, they were able to collect relevant data, analyze it, interpret it, and address the requirements of their strategic planning.

Anyone who watched the participants at work could only appreciate the profound importance and benefits of involving everyone throughout the evaluation process. For instance, at the one-day meeting for analyzing and interpreting the data, which the group called a "visioning session," participants began by letting several members review the history of the organization to provide a context for the day's work.

A local farmer, who direct-markets chemical-and-hormone-free beef, recalled the beginnings of the association: "We had an organizational meeting at the Carlton County Courthouse, and there was a speaker about lime and calcium application. That was about nine years ago, and 40 people attended." Other people added that the association has since established an annual "Harvest Festival" (a consumer outreach event), two farmer's markets, a "Chicken Bus" equipped as a mobile poultry processing plant, a bimonthly newsletter, educational seminars, and an annual tour of farms. One participant summarized the association's principle as follows: "Our premise is that a strong, local agriculture is crucial to maintaining a safe, secure, and healthy food supply; a diversified economy; and thriving rural communities."

Following this historical review, and before moving into the third task of the day, which was to analyze the data they had collected through surveys and interviews, the participants discussed the current state of their organization. It is interesting to note that the group felt it was important to talk not only about their organization's history but also about its current state of affairs in preparation for data analysis. This is the kind of important insight, with its attendant judgments, that is usually missed when data collection, analysis, and interpretation are treated as mechanical and expert-oriented processes that only a select few can accomplish.

With the historical and contemporary context of the Sustainable Farming Association reviewed, the participants broke into small groups to analyze and interpret the data collected (through surveys and interviews) from members, affiliated organizations, and nonmembers. Each five-person group analyzed and interpreted the same data. Then all participants got together as a group to discuss each subgroup's findings and interpretation in order to consider all perspectives and develop a document that encompassed the entire group's findings and interpretations of those findings. The above steps resulted in a strategic plan developed by all citizens interested in the Sustainable Farming Association, which included a vision and strategies for accomplishing the vision in the next five years.[38]

Finally, the group concluded their strategic planning processes by examining the implication of their new vision, focus areas, and strategies for how they do business. The implications and conclusions were identified through a group-facilitated process that addressed the question: "If the Board is serious about the commitments made in this strategic plan, how will it change the way we do our business?" This final process represented the board's commitment to successfully implementing its strategic plan.

Throughout the process, the hired consultant did exactly what she was supposed to do—facilitate active participation in the project by using methods that were appropriate for the purpose and setting.[39] The goal of the facilitator was to promote the people's individual and collective capacity to determine their own future—not to do that for them.

Just as a facilitator cannot correctly assess the past or the present for a group of people, neither can he or she determine the future, any more than a group can without every member's participation, which make diversity and inclusion imperative. Such inclusiveness means ensuring that all demographic, socio-economic, and ethic groups—especially the disenfranchised—are actively involved in every aspect of the work; it also means that all view points are considered when interpreting data since everyone sees life through his or her own lens that is colored by personal background, training, experiences, bias, interests, and so on. Involvement of all stakeholders (which can be enhanced through public meetings, workshops, conversations, and more) not only assures inclusion and diversity of opinions, but it also acknowledges the multiple ways of learning or perceiving things. Further, it builds ownership and interest in both the current work and future efforts.

It is only through a sincere consideration of all perspectives involving all interested citizens that one can get the most realistic interpretation of the world, which is critical, as author Paul Hawken noted in his book *The Ecology of Commerce,* because individuals, businesses, families, communities, countries and so on can be succeeding "according to conventional standards and still be violating profoundly important biological and natural systems."[40] Hawken went further to point out that the "natural world of sunlight, rainfall, and photosynthesis, of topsoil and coral reefs, of raptors and tropical fishes, of stamens and pistils and genes is a limit which can be circumvented only at the cost of the world itself," and argued (and we agree) that it "is only in the fullest context of the world itself as it is presented to us, and not as we manipulate it, that we may celebrate our humanity and create true prosperity."[41]

A sincere and holistic examination of the world around us can also make us more likely to acknowledge the fact that there are a lot of things we neither know nor understand as we interpret data. Data will only tell us so much—not everything. Once we understand what our findings mean and are mindful of what we do not know, we are ready to proceed in communicating and using the results of our evaluation, which is the subject of our next chapter.

5

COMMUNICATING AND USING EVALUATION FINDINGS

Unless people are informed about the results of an evaluation, how can those who need to make decisions and act on the findings know what the conclusions are? To be well utilized, the results of an evaluation must be appropriately communicated to the people who need to understand the findings. Assuring access to findings derived from an evaluation is therefore imperative.

An evaluation conducted in a participatory manner, with active involvement of all citizens throughout the process (as we advocate), has a head-start in this regard because everyone involved should be familiar with and interested in the evaluation. If an evaluation is done with the full participation of all interested citizens, and if these are the only people who need the information to make the necessary decisions, then those who need the information would have it whether or not the results were formally written down and reported. Such an evaluation is referred to as a "living evaluation."[42]

Having said this, however, one must realize that it is possible—even likely—that not all participants would know every detail about the findings. Further, evaluation findings tend to have far reaching implications for many people beyond those citizens who conducted the study. Therefore, the results must be communicated intentionally, explicitly, and strategically to the participants, as well as to other stakeholders, because it usually takes more than those directly involved in a given evaluation to fully and effectively use its conclusions, which brings us to the process of communication.

The Process of Communication

Communication entails disseminating information via some media in order to achieve one or more purposes, such as education, promotion, change in behavior or public policy, and so on. In its simplest form, communication involves *sender, message, channel,* and *receiver.* The message originates from the sender and travels through some channel to the receiver. In reality, however, human communication is more complex than a linear one-way model by which messages are transferred from a sender to a receiver via a channel. While relevant in a few cases, such a linear model does not accurately describe the vast majority of interpersonal communications "more accurately described by a convergence model in which the participants create and share information with one another to reach a mutual understanding."[43]

While approaches to interactive and nonlinear communication are more consistent with and suitable for sustainable development, different approaches have different uses. To develop an appropriate and effective communication strategy, however, all approaches must take the important elements of communication into account: (1) audience, (2) problem/need, (3) message, (4) channel, (5) gatekeepers, (6) message uncertainty, (7) noise and filters, (8) feedback, and (9) method and tools.[44]

Audience: Sustainable development has many audiences, all of which must be targeted one way or the other in the reporting of evaluation results. A group planning to share the findings of their evaluation must therefore think strategically about who comprises their intended audience because it is impossible to develop an appropriate communication strategy without first clarifying the target audience(s), which includes determining who needs to know what, why, when, and how.

Recall, if you will, that one of the steps in defining the objectives of an evaluation is to identify the questions various interested citizens want to ask. Beyond that, one must determine who needs to use the results of the evaluation and why, which translates into understanding the users' expectations. Explicitly characterizing these things helps assure that all relevant audiences are contacted and that the results are appropriately communicated to each.

The first task, then, is to identify and define the target audience(s). The next is to determine and record the important characteristics of each audience. Depending on what is to be communicated and how, it may be important to know such things as the kind of information required, socio-economic status, experience, age, gender, interest, philosophy, religion, educational background, occupation, political orientation of the audience, and their knowledge of and their attitude toward the subject and the messenger.

The idea is to learn what is relevant, and therefore necessary, in order to design the right message for a given audience and to communicate that message appropriately and effectively. Knowing the general background of an audience can help a group tailor both its message and method of communication to best accommodate the audience.

Another useful piece of information about members of an audience is what they like and what they don't. For example, we know from everyday experience that most people want to be recognized; to be treated in a friendly, fair way; and to be treated as equals. Most people want to gain or maintain such things as social status, comfortable beliefs, credibility, attention, wealth, praise, health, security, enjoyment, confidence, and so on. People like to be successful, creative, loved, famous, achievers, sociable, good, efficient, influential, up-to-date, as well as having fun, and satisfying their curiosity along the way. On the other hand, people generally like to avoid embarrassment, failure, indebtedness, illness, dependency, worry, doubts, domination, discomfort, and so on. No group of individuals, however, is a monolith.

What people like or dislike, accept or fear varies from person to person, culture to culture, setting to setting, and from one audience to another. To be successful, therefore, communication has to be done in ways that eliminate or reduce potential obstacles to hearing the results of an evaluation and the perceived risks of accepting the data at face value. This is difficult to do without knowing the audience. It is imperative to know and understand the intended audience if one is to effectively match the audiences' required information with one's need to share the results of a given evaluation.

Knowing the relative speed with which one target individual or community adopts a new idea as opposed to another is also important when communicating the results of an evaluation with the goal of affecting an overt behavioral change because people adopt innovations in a timed sequence. In turn, this sequence allows the classification of people into categories based on how quickly they adopt a new idea: innovator, early adopter, early majority, late majority, or laggard. There are important differences in socio-economic status, personality, and ability to communicate among those people who tend to adopt innovation early and those who adopt it late or not at all. The dominant attributes include being: adventuresome (innovators), respected (early adopter), deliberate (early majority), skeptical (late majority), and traditional (laggard).[45]

The differences among these categories suggest that different approaches be used for each in order to communicate effectively with a particular audience. Classifying the individuals of an audience (innovators, early adopters, early majority, late majority, and laggards) allows different channels of communication or messages to be aimed at each category with respect to its mental readiness to hear and accept new ideas.

By aggregating a heterogeneous audience into a series of relatively more homogeneous groups within the audience, one might be better able to communicate with the various groups with different strategies. For instance, one can appeal to innovators by showing that an idea was soundly tested and developed by credible scientists, whereas this approach may not be effective with the late majority or laggards, who will not adopt a new idea until they feel that most of the uncertainty about its performance has been removed. This part of the audience places greater credibility in the subjective experiences of their peers, which is conveyed to them through a trusted interpersonal network.[46]

Problem/Need: A problem or need exists when there is "an undesirable difference between 'wants' or norms and 'gets' or impact."[47] For instance, there is an environmental problem when there is an unwanted difference between some adverse environmental effects of a human activity and a desired future of healthy environment. Such a situation creates the need for information to be communicated in a way that reduces, if not eliminates, the dissonance between what a particular circumstance is and what someone or group wants it to be.

Clearly, compatibility of the message with the receiver's need for the information is an important factor. Perhaps it is obvious, but information that meets the perceived needs of the audience is most likely to be readily adopted and put to use. It is thus important to determine and clarify what needs to be communicated and how in order to develop the right message and the appropriate strategy to deliver that message if the need for the information is to be met. In doing this, one must consider both what information the audience needs to hear and what information the evaluators need to communicate based on their findings. In other words, one needs to ask the following questions: (1) What kind of information is needed to solve the identified problem? (2) What type of information is available from our evaluation results? and (3) How should it be presented in order to be heard, accepted, and acted on?

When evaluation is conducted in a participatory manner with the active involvement of all interested citizens, both needs (the kind of information gathered and the communication of that information) tend to be well matched. In determining what kind of communication is needed, one can start by revisiting the questions the evaluation was designed to answer and the results that were generated. In so doing, one determines the following: (1) the existing requirements for communication, (2) which of these requirements have to be met, (3) what the responsibilities of reporting the information are with respect to the different audiences, and (4) the different uses to which the evaluation findings may be put. Once an exhaustive list of the communication requirements and reporting responsibilities has been made, one can prioritize these things and decide which to meet and how. Oftentimes, however, it is neither possible nor even necessary to meet all the identified needs for a variety of reasons. So choices have to be made to do the best possible evaluation.

Message: Message refers to what one tells the receiver. Inherent in the message is the audience's response to the message or the outcome one wants to achieve as a result of the message. It is therefore important to be crystal clear about what the message is and the ultimate purpose of its delivery. Unless there is a clear and participatory definition of the message, it is difficult to communicate appropriately and effectively.

In defining a message, it is advisable to consider the relative advantage (or disadvantage) with which the audience may perceive it. Considering the potential advantages and disadvantages of the message will enable its presentation in a way that enhances its perceived advantage, which is important because a message perceived as an advantage has an easier time being adopted.[48]

The relative advantage of a message is not just financial or economic; other things, such as social approval or feeling of being socially and/or ethically responsible, may be equally, if not more, important to a particular audience. By one's knowing the results of an evaluation as well as one knows the audience (and vice versa), it is possible to highlight specific aspects or implications of the message in order to enhance its perceived relative advantage and thus its effectiveness.

Recognizing that an audience's perception of any message is colored by how the message is framed, including the words, symbols, and messenger used, a group planning to communicate the results of their evaluation is advised to plan carefully because how a message is framed inevitably affects how it is received. And the receiver's perception of the message or results of an evaluation affects how—or if—it is adopted and used.

A receiver-oriented approach to framing a message is therefore recommended. This approach entails taking into consideration how the receiver will react to the message to assure that the message has the desired meaning and outcome.

Characteristics of a message are also important. For instance, new ideas will be adopted most rapidly if they are perceived to have greater relative advantage than disadvantage, are compatible with the audience's perceptions, are testable, observable, and relatively simple and straightforward. Past research indicates that the above-mentioned qualities are the most important characteristics in explaining the rate at which a new idea or innovation is adopted.[49] To enhance the adoption of an evaluation's results, it is advisable to present them simply, understandably, and with immediate applicability that is compatible with the people's needs and circumstances.

Channel: A communication channel is the means by which a message gets from a sender to a receiver and vice versa. Communication channels can be categorized into: (1) mass media channels, such as the Internet, newspapers, radio, and television, which can be used by one or more senders to reach many divergent receivers simultaneously; and (2) interpersonal channels, which are one-on-one meetings or group meetings that typically involve a face-to-face interaction between two or more people, such as when neighbors meet or someone chats with an opinion leader or a salesperson.

Although mass media channels are the most rapid and efficient means of creating the awareness of an evaluation and/or its results among the general public, interpersonal channels are more effective in persuading people to accept a new idea and stimulating overt change in the behavior of individuals. Although most individuals do not evaluate a new idea or innovation on the basis of a scientific study of its consequences, such evaluations are relevant, nevertheless, especially to the first individuals who adopt the idea. Most people depend mainly on the explicitly subjective evaluation of a new idea as other people like themselves convey it to them. This overt subjectivity underscores the importance of interpersonal channels in the communicating of new and innovative ideas that result from an evaluation of some aspect of sustainable development.

Ultimately, the best practice is to use both the mass media and interpersonal channels in order to successfully reach various kinds of people and communicate most effectively at the various stages in the process of diffusing information. In other words, both communication channels (mass media and interpersonal) play different and important roles in the decision-making process when it comes to the ease with which a new and innovative idea is accepted and put into practice. For instance, people may become aware of new ideas, such as recycling and carpooling, for the first time from such mass media channels as television, radio, posters on the side of a mass-transit bus, and so on, but it is usually interpersonal communication that is most persuasive in getting people to adopt new ideas.

As discussed earlier in this chapter, people who are themselves innovators may accept a new idea communicated via mass media if they believe it is based on credible research. But this approach is not effective with people who are slow to adopt new ideas and who place the greatest credibility in the subjective experiences of peers, which is conveyed to them through interpersonal networks. Thus, the communication channel and the personal characteristics of the receiver interact to hasten or slow the rate with which a given personality type adopts a new idea. It is therefore advisable to use the interpersonal channel of communication when presenting complex ideas in an attempt to achieve overt behavioral change among noninnovative individuals.

Gatekeepers: Gatekeepers are the individuals situated between a sender and the receiver of a given message. A gatekeeper is any person who determines whether or not a particular message is to be sent, to which audience, and in what form. Examples of gatekeepers include messengers, producers, editors, directors, photographers, TV anchorpersons, and the viewer or listener (such as a parent) who can decide for others (such as children) what they are allowed to listen to or watch at a given point in time.

Message Uncertainty: A particular message may convey different things to different people. Thus, a sender or receiver can interpret the message in such a way as to create uncertainty with respect to its actual content. If words are not carefully chosen, or if they are improperly used, they can create a message fraught with uncertainty because of the different perceptions between a sender and receiver of what the message is *really* about and for whom it is *really* intended—which is the cause of many a rumor mill. Other elements of the communication process, such as channel, noise, gatekeepers, setting, and so on, can also create message uncertainty.

Message uncertainty can be reduced by: (1) choosing words that clarify (rather than confound) the intent of the message, (2) using variations in how the message is delivered, (3) having strategic redundancy, and (4) using and creating the "right" environment for effective communication and/or opportunities for learning.

Noise and Filters: Noise and filters are things that might disturb the message. Noise refers to anything happening in the background that can make the communication less effective or even ineffective. This loss of effectiveness may be due to actual noise or some other distraction, including the environment (physical, social, or psychological), or such things as someone being sick, worried, or absent minded. Filters, on the other hand, are those things that affect how the receiver hears the message, including culture, language, experience, gender, age, circumstances, predisposition to the information, and so on.

To successfully send a message, a sender needs to recognize and deal with the receiver's potential noises and filters. Each participant's noises and filters can be most easily recognized and overcome when participants are both senders and receivers in a dynamic and engaging process of mutual communication because people in such a circumstance not only build messages together but also listen together. Such interactive communication enables participants to know and appreciate one another's circumstances, expectations, needs, and challenges in communicating.

Feedback: Feedback, which is a process of returned communication between sender and receiver, is imperative in order for people to achieve consonance, balance, and congruity in their communication. Feedback from a receiver to a sender and vice versa helps assure accurate and successful communication because it enables the communicators to move toward mutual understanding, thus guiding their subsequent messages and behavior during communication. Without feedback, communication loses dynamism, which makes it difficult for people to determine facts and to communicate them effectively, which is a major problem with "top down" or nonparticipatory communication.

Method and Tools: There are many methods, tools, and media options for communicating the results of an evaluation. Examples include oral presentation, short courses, meetings, games, demonstrations, workshops, conferences, newspapers, television, movies, radio, computers, placards, leaflets, teleconferences, telephone, telegraph, satellite, fax, mailings, magazine, billboards, photograph, shows, fairs, music, commercials, neon signs, airplane writing, books, written reports, news releases, interviews, charts and graphics, e-mail, the World Wide Web, give aways (such as key chains, buttons, t-shirts, and pens with some kind of message on it), arts, rallies, and so on. Messages can also be delivered using comics, overhead projectors, video cameras, VCRs, clip arts, chalkboards, toys, bumper stickers, audiotapes, compact discs, laser discs, newsletters, sign language and body language (such as facial and hand expressions), games, and so forth.

Some methods, such as home visits, office calls, personal letters, facilitated self-training, personal investigation, or interviews, work well for communicating with individuals. On the other hand, demonstrations, field trials, workshops, fairs, lectures, group discussions, tours, field trips, role playing, drama, theater, simulation games, brainstorming, study teams, group meetings, teleconferences, judging, quiz games, and group presentation techniques (such as a panel, forum, and colloquium) are more appropriate for communicating to or within a group. While methods of mass communication, such as radio, newsletters, newspapers, magazines, bulletins, textbooks, posters, exhibits, information centers, movies, flyers, web pages, and so on are very useful for reaching many receivers simultaneously with the same message.

Creative expression, such as art, can be used as a means of individual or group expression and for interpreting information. One of us (Maser) once helped a national forest put on a week-long conference on the notion of ancient forests in an effort to engage local people in the process of forest management. Because ancient forest or old-growth forests, as they are also called, can only be characterized ecologically—not defined verbally or in writing, the conference had a scientific core. The scientific core did little or nothing, however, to approach, much less express, the spiritual dimensions of the local ancient forest that each person had secreted in his or her own heart.

To help the citizens express their feelings, their individual and collective spiritual connection with their local ancient forest, Maser had the local personnel of the U.S. Forest Service put up photographs of various places within that particular national forest that represented different ages along a continuum from young forest to very old forest. Each participant in the conference was then given a piece of paper and a pencil and asked to select the photograph that most resembled their notion of an ancient forest for each of the three or four different types of forest. Not everyone, however, was interested in the photographs.

If, therefore, the photographs held no interest for a particular participant, he or she could write a poem, tell a story on tape or write one on paper, sketch or paint a picture, or even bring in his or her own photograph. In this way, each participant could express his or her feelings in the way that worked best for that person, which allowed each person to feel they had been genuinely listened to, heard, and taken seriously because they were asked to participate up front in rewriting the forest management plan. Consequently, the conference far exceeded the Forest Service's expectations.

Special projects offer great opportunities for people to learn and share about a given subject or issue. In addition, political forms of communication, such as protests, picket lines, boycotts, public education, lobbying, strikes, rallies, and demonstrations, are also powerful means of communicating the results of an evaluation. For instance, organizations, like Greenpeace, sometimes use political means of communication to draw attention to certain issues in order to inform people and urge them to change public policy and/or their behavior.

It is unwise, therefore, to rely only on formal means such as written reports in communicating the vital results of an evaluation. If only one or two methods of communication are used, there is a risk of missing many people who cannot be reached by such methods, but might benefit from the evaluation results. Unfortunately, it too often happens that evaluation results end up in voluminous reports that very few people read.

A group involved in an evaluation would therefore be well advised to select and use an appropriate mix of communication methods and tools as part of an effective, participatory strategy for disseminating the results of their evaluation. Although we will not describe here all the methods and tools that can be used or how to use them appropriately, the following are some factors to keep in mind when deciding on which methods and tools to use:

1. Consider your audience and make sure you can reach the right people with the methods and tools you have chosen.

2. Consider your skills and resources and select methods and tools that match them. It would be futile, for instance, to choose a web-based method if you do not have the skill and/or resources to implement it.

3. Consider the audience and match the method to the needs, interests, characteristics, and communication behavior of your audience, such as their typical or preferred source of information and their innovativeness or willingness to accept and apply new ideas.

4. Consider the alternative options for communication that are available and the ability of the sender, be it you or your group, to use such techniques. What options do you really have? What is the feasibility of each option in the given circumstances?

5. Consider how visual presentations in graphics, charts, and so on can be used to enhance your communication with various audiences. Consider also your ability to use each of the available options and what would work best for a given type of data.

   For instance, data tables can be used to summarize quantitative data by tabulating statistics (for example, percentage, average, etc.) associated with relevant variables. Bar charts can be used to display distributions of categorical variables, such as gender, age, and occupation. Pie charts can be used to illustrate the distribution of a given indicator, where each slice of the pie represents a corresponding proportion or percentage of a specific subgroup relative to the whole group, which is made up of all slices and totals 100 percent. Maps, photographs, diagrams, and other forms of visual presentation can be used to effectively summarize qualitative data. We have all heard the saying "a picture is worth more than a thousand words."

   This said, a graphic representation has to be appropriate for the intended purpose because different types of graphics are useful for illustrating different types of relationships or patterns. In other words, you should use the one(s) that will effectively summarize and illustrate what you need to communicate. For instance, pie charts, and bar charts are useful for illustrating various parts of a whole (percentages), while maps are useful for comparing geographic characteristics of places, and curve graphs are useful for showing the relationship between or among variables or changes over time (time series).

With all of the above possibilities at hand, you might wonder where to begin. First you have to articulate what you want to show about any given aspect of your data and then choose or create a chart that illustrates the information you want to share. Then label the illustration completely and present using methods that will most effectively achieve the desired outcome.

6. Consider the cost and sophistication of the methods and tools you choose. They should be consistent with the prevailing circumstances, such as the type of project involved, the nature of communication called for, and participant's financial reality. In this regard, simplicity is an important factor because if simplicity is not accounted for, the chosen method or tool will most likely make dissemination of the evaluation results more complicated than necessary and may well lose part of the intended audience.

7. Consider timeliness with which the evaluation results are presented. This consideration is important because some methods and tools of communication allow the dissemination of evaluation results to be accomplished in a more timely fashion than others. Using such methods and tools is especially important when timing is critical.

8. Consider the effect of the communication process on the people's participation. People need to be involved. It is therefore important to use the methods and tools that

support or enhance participation rather than those that discourage it.

Regardless of the specific methods and tools chosen to disseminate information generated by a given evaluation, it is imperative that they are appropriately used to assure effectiveness because even the best method and tools in the world will be of little or no use if they are poorly or inappropriately implemented.[50]

Having mentioned "information" in the above paragraph, we think it wise to offer an observation made by professor Ulrich Nitsch who said that information is more often used to sell products or acquire influence, power, and money than it is to enhance humanity's long-term health, quality of life, and equality.[51] This, says Nitsch, is the environment people face when trying to communicate their sense of factually and ethically reasoned information about issues of sustainability. The purpose of information, Nitsch continues, is to give as many people as possible access to knowledge and to encourage them to take personal responsibility for how they treat the environment, including one another; it is not to direct people or to control them in politically correct thinking.

The most important aspect of communication, contends Nitsch, is the message itself, which is contained in the meaning of the words and symbols people use to share information. Concentrating on the content and meaning of the words and symbols directs our attention toward people's thoughts, feelings, and actions and diverts it away from the purely technical aspects of communication. It is, after all, we humans who give substance to the words and symbols through our interaction with the world around us wherein our experiences teach us the various meanings those words and symbols can convey. There is no such thing as an objective interpretation of information, not only because people are strictly subjective beings who cannot be objective but also because everything exists in constantly changing relationships. "Information," according to Nitsch, "is given its substance and its meaning by those who perceive it and by the context within which it is perceived." Thus, it is important as part of the communication strategy to carefully consider the information to be communicated (message), those who will perceive it (audience), the context, and so on, and then plan the necessary activities and/or tasks, including their sequence and timing, as well as who will perform them.

Communication Strategy

It may be useful to clearly articulate and clarify what you want to communicate, to whom, when, and how by using the following steps:[52]

1. Identify a *need, problem,* or *situation* that can be improved or corrected by the application of one or more of your evaluation finding(s).

2. Identify the *audience(s)* that need to be reached. List specific audiences that may be influenced or relate to the need, problem, or situation identified above. List the characteristics of each audience and their attitudes toward your topic and you.

3. Clearly state your *vision, goals,* and *objectives* as identified by your *desired outcome.* Make sure that your objectives are stated plainly in terms of expected outcomes, that primary and secondary goals are plainly identified, that your goals are both realistic enough to be achieved and challenging enough to demand your best effort in moving toward your shared vision.

4. List your basic *message(s).* Will the message(s) meet the identified need (step 1) and achieve the desired outcome (step 3)?

5. Identify potential *gatekeepers,* sources of *message uncertainty, filters, noise, opposition,* and so on. Describe how you will deal with each of the identified potential

sources of interference with your message in order to assure accurate and effective communication.

6. List the *communication methods, media,* and *channels* you would employ to deliver your message(s). Consider those that would be most effective in achieving the desired response and/or outcomes? Consider characteristics of the audience, available resources, relevant networks, and so on.

7. Explain the *sequence* and *timing* of your communication activities. Clearly identify who performs each of the above activities, when, and how.

8. Consider the *cost* of different elements of the communication work. Is it *cost-effective*? Can I *afford* it? How will I *fund* this?

9. Describe how you will know whether you have achieved the desired responses and/or outcomes. Suggest some means by which you would measure success. Be sure your evaluation criteria are linked to your vision, goals, and objectives.

Ultimately, however, data must be presented as a basis for informed conversation and decision making that involves all concerned, not in ways that will force certain decisions on people or overlook other alternatives. In other words, communication is not a mechanism for delivering evaluation results to a passive audience.

It may not be possible, however, to involve everyone in all phases of an evaluation and thus guarantee everyone's ownership of the results in all steps of the process. Nevertheless, communication of evaluation results should be seen as contributing to a shared process of learning and informed public debate. Neither goals nor the means to achieving them should be taken for granted.

It often happens, however, that some group or individual rushes out to "communicate" a given finding with the sole purpose of convincing others to accept certain prescriptions which this group or individual sees as an appropriate means of achieving a certain goal. The problem with this approach is that it assumes that everyone already agrees with the goal and all that is needed is to convince people we have the best idea regarding the means to achieve that goal. Needless to say this is usually ineffective.

Evaluation results should be used in ways that enable people to arrive at good socially negotiated agreements that promote sustainable development. This is important because people create their own reality through interactions. And as Jim Rugh noted, if an evaluation is done with the full participation of all stakeholders, it can be a living evaluation. By living evaluation, Rugh means that those who need to know what the results of an evaluation are will find out as the evaluation is conducted, whether or not the results are written in a formal report. The important thing is that the relevant findings are communicated to those who need the information in order to make decisions and take actions. Moreover, the results should be communicated in such a way that barriers to gaining the needed information and making the required decisions are either removed or at least minimized.[53]

DESIGNING AND IMPLEMENTING AN EVALUATION PLAN

We hope to accomplish two things in this final chapter. First, we do our best to provide a practical guide for designing a customized evaluation plan. Second, we discuss some common problems that are generally encountered when implementing an evaluation project and offer helpful suggestions on how to get around such problems. We begin with a simple guide for people who want to formulate their evaluation plan.

Creating a Customized Evaluation Plan

The following steps are suggested as a guide for people to follow in developing a customized plan for evaluating whatever sustainable development project or phenomenon they are interested in:

Step 1, principles of sustainable development: Start by discussing your group's guiding principles and philosophy. Outline in simple and practical terms how they relate to the phenomenon you want to evaluate. How should your guiding principle influence your evaluation?

Step 2, purpose of the evaluation: Determine and agree (as a group) on why you want to conduct the evaluation in the first place. The reason for evaluation is to meet specifically identified needs; to provide answers to important questions. Keeping in mind the diverse audiences who will need to use the information; therefore, participants should outline clear, easily understood questions to which they are interested in finding answers.

This exercise will help you define what needs or problems you hope to meet or solve by conducting this evaluation. It will also help you examine and clarify differences in opinions regarding the purpose of the proposed evaluation.

Step 3, determining what to evaluate: To ensure the group agrees on what is to be evaluated, outline the questions you, as a group, have decided to answer, which goes beyond simply identifying and listing all possible questions that can be evaluated. It means that members of a group must agree, as a whole, on which questions the group really wants to answer. In other words, the group has to decide—in a participatory fashion— what to evaluate based on such factors as: (1) information needed, (2) group priorities, and (3) available resources (for example, budget, time, skill).

Step 4, indicators or variables to monitor: Identify and choose specific pieces of information to monitor or measure that will tell you what is happening with regard to your stated goals and objectives. For instance, if you, as a group, want to know how healthy individual members of your community are, you have to also agree on what you consider appropriate indicators of health since there are many variables that can be used, such as temperature, weight, cholesterol level, blood pressure, and so on. It is therefore necessary to reach a consensus around specific variables or indicators that will measure what you want to evaluate.

Step 5, approaches to evaluation: Consider, as a group, alternative approaches to evaluation and then select one(s) that will best meet the purpose of your evaluation. Be sure to choose an evaluation approach that is scientifically valid, appropriate for your situation, *and* harmonious with the principles of sustainable development.

Step 6, evaluation design: What are your options with regard to *sources* and *timing* of data collection? Consider, as a group, the various evaluation designs that you can have, and then choose the option(s) that will give you the most credible result.

Step 7, population and sampling: Are you going to study the entire population or a sample? If you decide to study a sample, what method will you use? What are some pertinent characteristics of your chosen population?

Step 8, collecting data: Based on the question being asked and the phenomenon being studied, decide what kind of data will be used. Decide how you will gather accurate, useful, and complete information to answer the question(s) posed. Explore the options available for collecting data and choose the one(s) that are most feasible and appropriate. What are the measurement strategies or instruments involved? What are the procedures for assessing validity and reliability? What qualitative and/or quantitative data collection procedures will be used?

Step 9, analyzing data: Decide the qualitative and/or quantitative data-analysis techniques that will be used for your evaluation. What techniques and tools will be used to analyze information? What purpose will each technique and/or tool serve (for example, description, examination of differences, or examination of relationships)?

Step 10, summarizing and interpreting findings: How best can you summarize, analyze, and interpret the information collected?

Step 11, communicating findings: Most efforts in sustainable development have numerous stakeholders and audiences, all of whom must be included in receiving the evaluation's results. How will you determine who needs to know what, when, and how? How will you communicate the results to potential users of such information? What methods of communication and which media will you use to disseminate the results based on your understanding of the potential users' characteristics, information needs, and expectations.

Step 12, participation: In formulating an evaluation plan, as much emphasis must be placed on active participation, diversity and, inclusion of all interested parties as on all other aspects of the evaluation project. How will you assure active participation of various citizens in all aspects and stages of the evaluation process? How will you include the different perspectives of all participants?

Step 13, operational timing: How will you schedule the implementation of your evaluation plan?

Step 14, budget: What will the evaluation plan cost? How will you fund it?

Having outlined a list of steps to be taken in setting up your evaluation, we now turn to potential constraints.

Potential Constraints and Suggested Solutions

Potential constraints to the proper planning of an evaluation to assess projects concerned with sustainable development include: (1) lack of vision and leadership, (2) lack of coordination, (3) lack of appreciation of basic sustainable development principles and concepts, (4) lack of skilled human resources, (5) lack of financial resources, (6) lack of time, (7) incomplete cost accounting, (8) "top-down" or nonparticipatory programming, (9) cultural issues, and (10) the sometimes difficult task of balancing thoroughness with political "reality." Below, you will find a brief discussion of these problems and some suggestions on how to overcome them.

Lack of Vision and Leadership

Defining a vision and committing it to paper goes against our training as individuals because it must be stated as a positive in the positive, something we are not used to doing. Stating a positive in the positive means stating what we mean directly. For example, a local community has an urban growth boundary that it wants to keep within certain limits, which can be stated in one of two ways: (1) we want our urban growth boundary to remain within a half a mile from where it is now situated (a positive stated as a positive), or (2) we don't want our urban growth boundary to extend beyond a half mile from where it is now (a negative that one is attempting to state as a positive).

Further, to save our planet and human society, as we know it, we must be willing to risk changing our thinking in order to have a wider perception of the world and its possibilities, to validate one another's points of view or frames of reference. The world can be perceived with greater clarity when it is observed simultaneously from many points of view. Such conception requires open-mindedness in a collaborative process of intellectual and emotional exploration of that which is and that which might be, the result of which is a shared vision of a possible future.

Two sayings are pertinent here: If you don't know where you're going, any path will take you there, and if you stand for everything, you soon find that you stand for nothing. Would you for a moment consider flying in a commercial airplane if the pilot did not know where he or she was going, how much fuel was aboard, and roughly when you would arrive? Even nomadic hunters, gatherers, and herders knew where they were going; their livelihood—and their survival—depended on it.

Without a vision, we take "potluck" in terms of where we will end up, which was Alice's dilemma when she met the Cheshire cat in Lewis Carroll's *Alice's Adventures in Wonderland.*[54] Alice asked the Cheshire cat:

> "Would you tell me, please, which way I ought to go from here?"
>
> "That depends a good deal on where you want to get to," said the Cat.
>
> "I don't much care where—" said Alice.
>
> "Then it doesn't matter which way you go," said the Cat.
>
> "—so long as I get somewhere," Alice added as an explanation.
>
> "Oh, you're sure to do that," said the Cat, "if you only walk long enough."

The movie *Spartacus,* which depicts the true story of a Roman slave who as a boy of thirteen had been sold into slavery, is an excellent illustration of the power of a collective vision. Bought as a young man, Spartacus was taken to a highly organized school, where he was forced to learn fighting and become a gladiator. There was a revolt early in his career, however, and he, along with his fellow gladiators, escaped.

For a time, they ran roughshod over the countryside, disorganized and out of control. They robbed, raped, and murdered the Roman gentry and encouraged their slaves to join the growing mob. But Spartacus was uncomfortable with the out-of-control mob because he recognized that it had simply become what it was against; it had become like the Romans. He therefore organized the slaves into an army that would fight its way across Italy to the sea and escape.

In 71 BC, Spartacus led his army in an uprising. Now a highly organized fighting machine that opposed Roman rule, Spartacus' army had become a dangerous, out-of-control cancer (by Roman standards) that threatened the Roman sense of superiority, because it was, after all, just an army of slaves. Although the slaves twice defeated the Roman legions, they were finally conquered by General Marcus Licinius Crassus after a long siege and battle in which they were surrounded by and had to simultaneously fight three Roman legions.

The battle over, Crassus faces the thousand survivors seated on the ground as an officer shouts: "I bring a message from your master, Marcus Licinius Crassus, Commander of Italy. By command of his most merciful Excellency, your lives are to be spared. Slaves you were, and slaves you remain. But the terrible penalty of crucifixion has been set aside on the single condition that you identify the body or the living person of the slave called Spartacus."

After a long pause, Spartacus stands up to identify himself. Before he can speak, however, Antoninus leaps to his feet and yells, "I am Spartacus!" Immediately, another man stands and yells, "No, I'm Spartacus!" Then another leaps to his feet and yells, "No, I'm Spartacus!" Within minutes, the whole slave army is on its feet, each man yelling "I'm Spartacus!"

Each man, by standing, was committing himself to death by crucifixion. Yet their loyalty to Spartacus, their leader, was superseded only by their loyalty to the vision of themselves as free men, the vision that Spartacus had inspired—and Crassus could not take away, even with the threat of death by crucifixion. The vision was so compelling that, having tasted freedom, they willingly chose death over once again submitting to slavery. And they were, to a man, crucified along the road to Rome. But by withholding their obedience from Crassus, they remained free because slavery requires that the oppressed submit their obedience to the oppressor.

Although a vision may begin as an intellectual idea, at some point it becomes enshrined in one's heart as a palpable force that defies explanation. It then becomes impossible to turn back, to accept that which was before, because to do so would be to die inside. Few, if any, forces in human affairs are as powerful as a shared vision of the heart. Consider Mahatma Gandhi's inspired fight to free India from British rule.

In its simplest, intellectual form, a shared vision asks: What do we want to create? Why do we want to create it? Beyond that, it becomes the focus and energy to bring forth that which is desired, because, as John F. Kennedy said, "Those who anticipate the future are empowered to create it," which is similar to Gandhi's statement: "The future depends on what we do in the present." It is also similar to Franklin Delano Roosevelt's statement: "The only limit to our realization of tomorrow will be our doubts of today." Alas, few people know what a vision, goal, or objective is; how to create them; how to state them; or how to use them as guidelines for sustainable development.

A statement of *vision* is a general declaration that describes what a particular person, group of people, agency, or nation is striving for. A vision is like a "vanishing point," the spot on the horizon where the straight, flat road on which you are driving disappears from view over a gentle rise in the distance.

As long as you keep that vanishing point in focus as the place you want to go, you are free to take a few side trips down other roads and always know where you are in relation to where you want to go, your vision. It is necessary to have at hand a dictionary and a thesaurus when crafting a vision statement because it must be as precise as possible. After all, through it you must say what you mean *and* mean what you say.

Gifford Pinchot, the first chief of the U.S. Forest Service, had a vision of protected forests that would produce commodities for people in perpetuity. In them he saw the "greatest good for the greatest number in the long run." Through his leadership, he inspired this vision as a core value around which everyone in the new agency could, and did, rally for almost a century.

In a more recent example, the second author (Maser) spoke in 1989 to a Nation of First Canadians who owned a sawmill in central British Columbia. He had been asked to discuss how a coniferous forest functions, both above- and belowground, so that the First Canadians could better understand the notion of productive sustainability, something they were greatly concerned about. After he spoke, a contingent from the British Columbia provincial government told the First Canadians what they could and could not do in the eyes of the government. The government officials were insensitive at best. The First Canadians tried in vain to tell the officials how they felt about their land and how they were personally being treated. Both explanations fell on deaf ears.

After the meeting was over and the government people left, Maser explained to the First Canadians what a vision is, why it is important, and how to create one. In this case, they already knew in their hearts what they wanted; they had a shared vision, but they could not articulate it in a way that the government people, whose dealings with the First Canadians were strictly intellectual, could understand.

With Maser's help, they committed their feelings to paper as a vision statement for their sawmill in relation to the sustainable capacity of their land and their traditional ways. They were thus able to state their vision in a way that the government officials could understand, and it became their central point in future negotiations.

In contrast to a vision, a *goal* is a general statement of intent that remains until it is achieved, the need for it disappears, or the direction changes. Although a goal is a statement of direction, which may be vague and is not necessarily expected to be accomplished, it does serve to further clarify the vision statement. A goal might be stated as "My goal is to see Athens, Greece."

An *objective,* on the other hand, is a specific statement of intended accomplishment. It is attainable, has a reference to time, is observable and measurable, and has an associated cost. The following are additional attributes of an objective: (1) it starts with a verb; (2) it specifies a single outcome or result to be accomplished; (3) it specifies a date by which the accomplishment is to be completed; (4) it is framed in positive terms; (5) it is as specific and quantitative as possible and thus lends itself to evaluation; (6) it specifies only "what, where," and "when" and avoids mentioning "why" and the "how"; and (7) it is product oriented.

Consider the previous goal: "My goal is to see Athens, Greece." Let's now make it into an objective: "I will see Athens, Greece, on my 21st birthday." The stated objective is action oriented: I will see. It has a single outcome: seeing Athens, Greece. It specifies a date: my 21st birthday, and it is framed in positive terms: I will see. It lends itself to evaluation of whether or not the stated intent has been achieved, and it clearly states "what," "where," and "when." Finally, it is product or outcome oriented: to see a specific place.

As you strive to achieve such an objective, you must accept and remember that *your objective is fixed, as though in concrete, but the plan to achieve the objective must remain flexible and changeable.* A common human tendency, however, is to change the objective—devalue it—if it cannot be reached in the chosen way or by the chosen time. It is much easier, it seems, to devalue an objective than it is to change an elaborate plan that has shown it will not achieve the objective as originally conceived.

It is important to understand what is meant by vision, goal, and objective because collectively they tell you where you are going, the value of getting there, and the probability of success. Too often, however, people "sleeve shop." Sleeve shopping is going into a store to buy a jacket and deciding which jacket you like by the price tag on the sleeve.

The alternative to sleeve shopping is to first determine what you want by the perceived value and purpose of the outcome. Second, you must make the commitment to pay the price, whatever it is. Third, you must determine the price of achieving the outcome. Fourth, you must figure out how to fulfill your commitment—how to pay the price—and *make a commitment to keep your commitment*. And fifth, you must act on it.

Alexander the Great, the ancient Greek conqueror, provides an excellent example of knowing what one wants and how to achieve it. When he and his troops landed by ship on a foreign shore that he wanted to take, they found themselves badly outnumbered. As the story goes, he sent some men to burn the ships and then ordered his troops to watch the ships burn, after which he told them: "Now we win or die!"

The above story brings us to the notion of leadership. "As we evolve," notes Sufi teacher Pir Vilayat Inayat Khan, "we're able to transform the situation and the people around us by helping them to fulfill their purpose. Our purpose is to enlist the purpose of other people. That is really the secret of leadership." Why, then, are most shared community visions not implemented, even when they are touted as a success story? Community visions are often not implemented even though a community can, through a visioning process: (1) better understand the core values of its citizenry and use them as a basis for planning, (2) identify the trends and forces affecting the community, and (3) articulate a wide-angle picture in time and space to guide short-term decisions in relationship to long-term outcomes and initiatives.

Why is no action taken? Do people know they are going to all the trouble and expense of participating in a visioning exercise just to have it committed to paper? Are the personal behavioral constraints necessary to accomplish the goals too frightening socially, too restrictive ecologically, and hence too expensive economically in the short term?

What happens to the sense of urgency that promulgates the vision in the first place? Are there too many self-centered special-interest groups with enough political clout to render the vision impotent? Do too many people commute to the community to work but choose to live somewhere else and therefore were not interested in a vision for the city? Are too many of the business leaders, such as homebuilders and developers, more interested in making all the money they can immediately, so they can retire somewhere else and not live with the consequences of their actions? Were there no leaders of sufficient moral courage and political will to shepherd the vision through the maelstrom of change and its requirement of self-restraint?

If the reason for inaction is none of the above, can it be that the people simply lacked the conceptual framework that will allow them to understand the positive consequences of a shared vision for the present generation as well as the future? Consider that after Galileo had invented the telescope to study the heavens, he invited his contemporaries to peer through it and see for themselves the evidence that would overturn the conventional wisdom concerning the planets and stars. Many declined, however, because in their closed minds what Galileo was saying was impossible; so they refused to look, which, unfortunately, too often validates a comment by English statesman David Lloyd George: "It is always too late, or too little, or both. And that is the road to disaster."

If this is the mindset of your local political leaders, what is the point of going through the pain and expense of giving birth to a vision if it is simply left to gather dust in some city, county, or state office, which says nothing about betraying the time the citizens donated, the expenditure of their tax dollars, their trust in the process, and their expectations for the outcome. Would they have been willing to pay for the process and participate in it if they had known nothing would come of it? Probably not. The critical question is: Where was the leadership?

The lack of civic leadership is a problem not unique to any given community, as evidenced by the fact that the single most common criticism of the community visioning processes is the lack of successful follow-through? This reticence to deal honestly with a shared vision makes it worth repeating part of Winston Churchill's speech to the British Parliament in 1935, as he saw with clear foreboding the onrushing threat of Nazi Germany to international peace:

> When the situation was manageable it was neglected, and now that it is thoroughly out of hand we apply too late the remedies which then might have effected a cure. There is nothing new in the story . . . It falls into that long, dismal catalogue of the fruitlessness of experience and the confirmed unteachability of mankind. Want of foresight, unwillingness to act when action would be simple and effective, lack of clear thinking, confusion of counsel until the emergency comes, until self-preservation strikes its jarring gong—these are the features which constitute the endless repetition of history.[55]

"If you build castles in the air," wrote Henry David Thoreau, "your work need not be lost. That is where they should be. Now put the foundations under them." The problem faced by communities is one of foundations and, as such, often resides not only with the visioning process itself but also with a lack of leadership to ensure a true, freely participatory visioning process and adequate follow-through into the implementation phase and beyond.

If implementation is not actively linked with completion of the visioning process itself, the chances of achieving the vision are slim at best for the following reasons: (1) a community never develops an action plan; (2) a community develops an action plan but omits important interested parties; (3) a community never implements its action plan; and (4) a community fails to monitor progress in implementing its action plan. Again, leadership is the key to both a successful visioning process and the successful implementation of the vision, because, as American humorist Will Rogers noted: "Even if you're on the right track, you'll get run over if you just sit there."

Lack of Coordination

Although people are generally good about cooperating with one another, cooperation without coordination is an empty cup. It is imperative that people both cooperate and coordinate with one another if evaluating a community project dealing with sustainable development is to be carried to its conclusion in a meaningful way.

In this regard, it is advisable to identify one or more person(s) responsible for the coordination of any given evaluation. Further, it is helpful to clearly determine and itemize all the tasks or work items necessary for conducting the evaluation successfully; and specify who will do what part when and how. Finally, all the stakeholders (especially those actively involved in the evaluation) must plan and agree on how the various parts of the project would be pooled together as an integrated whole; and how the various players would work with the project coordinator(s) to assure coordination.

We have all heard the quibble about a job that *everybody* thought *somebody* would do, but *nobody* did it even though *anybody* could have done it. A group can avoid this and other problems associated with lack of coordination not only by eliminating confusion through clarity of tasks and responsibilities, but also by making coordination strategies an integral part of their work plan.

Lack of Appreciation of Basic Sustainable Development Principles and Concepts

As discussed earlier in this book, there are important principles, concepts, guidelines, and frameworks of sustainable development that people interested in evaluating sustainable development must be conscious of. A good understanding of these basic principles and concepts is essential for appropriately evaluating projects or phenomenon that deal with sustainable development.

This understanding is important because the main factor that separates evaluation of sustainable development from other kinds of evaluation is the degree to which the philosophy and method of evaluation considers and reflects the principles of sustainable development.

Further, it is advisable that citizens keep abreast of relevant issues and subjects concerning sustainable development in order to enhance their ability to understand and evaluate whatever project or phenomenon they are interested in. This calls for use of a variety of methods to stay informed, such as media coverage, town meetings, professional conferences, electronic means (for example, e-mail, list serve, chat rooms), and word of mouth.

Against this background, it is pertinent to note that things are rapidly changing and constantly evolving, which makes keeping up with new developments imperative. In addition, the need to separate reliable information from false or useless information demands a certain level of verification on the part of the user *before* he or she relies on any new information, idea, or novel method.

Lack of Skills

Lack of skills necessary for planning and conducting a given evaluation project can be a challenge. The level and type of skills needed to plan and execute specific evaluation protocols differ from project to project. The more complex, specialized, or technical an evaluation is, the more highly skilled, trained, or experienced personnel need to be. People thus frequently feel that they do not have the skills, training, or experience necessary to conduct some aspect of a given evaluation, such as planning, data collection, data analysis, and/or writing reports.

Potential solutions to the above problem include: (1) letting the more skilled persons in the group coordinate the process and coach others, (2) rotating responsibilities as a way of drawing on a wider range of abilities, (3) using people who may not be highly skilled but who have the interest and ability to learn, (4) providing specialized training to participants in relevant areas, such as facilitation, data analysis, and documentation to enhance their abilities and confidence, and (5) using information in books to build skills within a community, project, or organization.[56] Additionally, knowledgeable individuals and groups, both within and without the community, can be engaged to help build the necessary skills of other individuals and the community as a whole.

Often, available human resources are underutilized. This is especially the case when available resources are not readily apparent, as illustrated by the following story about the wealth of experience, skill, and volunteer potential that was largely untapped in Fort Collins, Colorado, when one of the authors (Ukaga) was the Managing Director of the International Institute for Sustainable Development at Colorado State University.

Shortly after the Institute was established, it had a great need for people with skills, training, and experience in a variety of disciplines to work on projects doing research, training, program planning, and so on. At one time, the Institute needed water engineers, civil engineers, chemical engineers, public health professionals, food and nutrition experts, medical doctors, business economists, extension specialists, agricultural economists, rural sociologists, and social workers for just one particular project. We tried to use faculty and students from the relevant departments with mixed results.

As Ukaga was running around recruiting professors, sometimes directly and sometimes through their deans and department heads, he ran into a retired professor who not only volunteered to work on this project, but as a former vice president of the University was able to also link the Institute with some more additional retired professors who played critical roles in implementing the project. After this experience, two things became clear: (1) there often is a substantial pool of highly experienced, readily available people who are willing to work, generally easier to access, and more cost-effective than the usual sources one is inclined to tap and (2) these people are not readily obvious, which is part of the reason they tend to be ignored.

Nevertheless, there are always more skilled people available to participate in a given community or on a particular project than are readily apparent. Finding them calls not only for being open to nontraditional sources of skilled and talented people but also for being aggressive, persistent, and creative in identifying and using those who are willing to participate. Nearby organizations, schools, and colleges are a few of the many potential sources of skilled personnel for evaluation projects.

Finally, it is important to stress that even though some people may feel they lack the skills, training, or experience necessary to conduct a given evaluation, there are three reasons everyone can participate:

1. It is more important that everyone participates than that everyone be highly skilled. When everyone is at the table, each participant brings certain skills and experiences—which are often complimentary to one another. In the end, therefore, the totality of the skills and experiences available within the group is usually more than sufficient to do the participants' collective job.

2. With gentle coaching, even those with little or no skills can learn to do a sound evaluation.

3. Citizens can seek and use outside expertise when needed in planning and implementing their evaluation project, which, in fact, should be encouraged. What is not good, is the erroneous notion that ordinary citizens cannot participate in an evaluation—that evaluation is something to be done by outside "experts" or a few "skilled" insiders.

Lack of Financial Resource

There are usually some costs associated with evaluation projects, such as the cost of necessary human and material resources. In participatory evaluation, the cost of personnel can be reduced drastically or eliminated all together by using citizen volunteers.

Similarly, a lot of the costs associated with evaluation materials and equipment can be eliminated or reduced through in-kind contributions of various things needed for the evaluation, such as people's time, writing materials, refreshments, office space, stationary, paper work, data collection, and processing equipment. As the old saying goes, a penny saved is a penny earned. Other cost-cutting measures include: avoiding waste, focusing only on what is essential—in other words, do not waste money on "extras."

Perhaps, the most important thing is to be realistic in planning an evaluation project. On one end of the spectrum, you might find citizens who feel they lack the resources to undertake an evaluation project. Such a feeling can lead them to *do nothing*. On the other end of the spectrum are citizens who feel they can do anything, even to the point of being overly optimistic or outright unrealistic. It is advisable for citizens to plan evaluations that are both effective and useful in answering the questions they want answered and are affordable and realistic. Additionally, citizens should seek sponsorships, grants, and leverages from a variety of public and of private sources as possible solutions to the lack of financial resources.

Being thrifty also helps a group overcome the problem of limited resources. In the spirit of sustainable development, it is imperative that you *reduce, reuse,* and *recycle* resources as much as possible, without compromising the quality of your evaluation. For instance, you can limit the use of paper to only that which is necessary by printing the reports, and then use both sides of the paper, as well as reusing paper and envelopes when feasible.

Lack of Time

Evaluation takes time. How much time depends in part on the questions the evaluation is seeking to answer, the evaluation approach or methodology employed, the tools and equipment being used, the nature of what is being studied, and the personnel invested in the effort. The fact that any evaluation would take some time (whether small or large) is not the problem. The problem is that people seldom allocate time specifically to evaluation-type activities as an integral part of their normal routine. This is partly because people are busy with other things they probably perceive as more important and/or urgent and partly because people perceive evaluation-related activities as burdensome and something they simply do not have time for. But, this need not be the case because people can overcome potential problems of insufficient time if the group or organization is committed to the evaluation processes to such a degree that their commitment would make them find the time needed to conduct the evaluation.[57]

Other potential solutions for a lack of time include:

- Using existing opportunities, such as adapting previously or routinely scheduled meetings to the needs of your evaluation work rather than creating additional time-consuming procedures

- Incorporating the evaluation as an integral part of the regular routine or process of any community project or activity and thus insure by design that time would be allocated for evaluation

- Being sensitive and responsive to needs and schedules of participants, which would assure that evaluation activities be conducted at times that are convenient and appropriate

- Focusing the evaluation on important and necessary work to be done in order to avoid wasting time on unnecessary or redundant work

- Encouraging people to make time for evaluation by demonstrating that a given evaluation is necessary and would be a useful exercise—because people tend to make time for what is important to them

- Selecting someone or a team of people to act as facilitator(s) and coordinate the project

Incomplete Cost Accounting

There are always present and future costs of various kinds associated with various levels or layers of any given phenomenon or area one may be interested in evaluating. In agriculture, for instance, there are costs (such as aquifers polluted by fertilizers and the effects of herbicides and pesticides on human health and the ecosystem) that are not routinely recognized. By the same token, our current fossil-fuel based economy has hidden costs, such as the military, political, economic, social, and ecological costs of securing the energy needed to maintain this system.

As illustrated by these two examples, there are costs associated with everything, and there is a general tendency to avoid counting or recognizing their full costs. There are many reasons for this, including "shortsightedness," which does not allow people to look beyond their narrow interests or immediate concerns, the procedural and resource constraints to calculating such costs, and the fact that some stakeholders may prefer to "externalize" as many costs as possible because they think it is in their economic and/or political interest to do so.

Despite such constraints to full cost accounting, one must always be aware that nothing is free. Whatever decision is made, there is a cost of some kind attached to it, both in the present and in the future. For example, in 1837, the 24-foot-high Edwards Dam was built across the Kennebec River in the state of Maine.[58] The 917-foot-wide dam was built 40 miles inland from the Atlantic Ocean to supply power to the mills that rose along the river's banks. The cost of the dam was 162-year blockage of striped bass, Atlantic salmon, herring, shad, and other fish from reaching their spawning grounds upstream from the dam. But in 1837 the fishery was so rich that early colonists grew weary of eating fish, and probably did not consider what the loss of so rich a fishery might mean to the generations of the future.

In 1997, the Federal Energy Regulatory Commission decided, against the wishes of the owners, that the Edwards Dam should be removed for the good of the environment. Contractors completed the removal of the timber, stone, and concrete structure on October 8, 1999, a little more than three months after the dam was breached.

With the dam gone, gazing at the Kennebec River from its high banks in Augusta is like looking back in time more than a century and a half. Now Coon's Rock rises near the left bank of the river, as Benedict Arnold may have noticed when he traveled through in the late 1700s; and the flat, gravelly Cushnoc Island is again in view as it was when colonial fisherman filled barrels at a time with Atlantic salmon from the river. Atlantic salmon have returned to the spawning grounds once denied them by Edwards Dam, and striped bass have come back in large numbers, as have their food, alewives, which also swim upstream from the sea.

The dam had costs, which included the financial cost of constructing it, as well as the impairment of the river ecosystem of which the fishery is an example. By the same token, the revived fishery and the other advantages of removing the dam also have costs, which include the loss of whatever goods, services, and revenue the dam had provided all those years. So any group involved in the evaluation of sustainable development should think about such costs in a relatively broad and comprehensive fashion and then determine what to include and where to stop based, among other things, on their objective, the scope of project, and what is realistically possible given available resources.

"Top-down" or Nonparticipatory Programming

Evaluation of sustainable development should be participatory—meaning that all legitimate stakeholders should be intentionally involved in a collaborative process that: (1) enables citizens to construct contextually meaningful knowledge, (2) engenders the personal and structural capacity to act on that knowledge, and (3) seeks action that contributes to improvements in the evaluation context.[59]

Participatory evaluation seeks to be "politically democratizing" and is rooted in valuing: (1) practitioner knowledge, experience, and utilization; (2) fair, reciprocal, and equitable relationships in inquiry; and (3) inclusiveness, social justice, and democratic pluralism.[60] But participatory evaluation often comes against the hard reality of habit and history, where autocratic, "top-down" or non-participatory programming is the norm.

When things are traditionally done in a top-down fashion, people do not easily think or plan in a participatory manner. The challenge for citizens planning to conduct an evaluation in such settings is first to recognize the problem and then to work hard to overcome it so participatory evaluation can, in fact, take place. Overcoming this habit is easier said than done, however, because old habits and traditions are difficult to break. As such, constant attention must be paid to various dimensions of participation, including:

Control: Who is controlling the evaluation? Who, for instance, decides the questions to ask and the data to collect? Who makes meaning of the results? Is the agenda, process, and meaningful decision-making authority controlled by the citizens or by other people (for example, researchers, politicians, the elite, special interest groups, and so on)?

Citizen involvement: Who is selected for participation? Does the evaluation engage only a few relatively homogenous, primary stakeholders or are all legitimate stakeholders involved? Is diversity maximized?

Depth of participation: Are participants deeply involved in the evaluation or are they merely being consulted? Are the members of the community fully and actively involved in all aspects of the evaluation from start to finish?

It is important to recognize that participatory evaluation does not just happen by accident or luck. It takes intentional planning and hard work to initiate, practice, and a vow of resilience to institutionalize a participatory approach to evaluation. The following story illustrates the challenge people face in trying to make their approach more participatory.

The program is the Integrated Rural Development Program of the Nigerian National Youth Service Corps, which is a community development effort designed to: (1) help improve the living standards of Nigerian rural communities and (2) redirect the energies of the Nigerian National Youth Service Corps by using the enormous human potential available to the Nigerian National Youth Service Corps (through the one-year voluntary services provided by most Nigerians upon graduation from college/university) to facilitate sustainable development, especially in rural communities. Specific objectives of this program are to:

- Alleviate poverty
- Raise agricultural production and productivity
- Improve the quality and availability of the water supply
- Improve primary health care and control disease
- Ensure a better educated population
- Support appropriate social programs
- Restore and/or maintain ecological balance and integrity across the country
- Stem rural to urban migration
- Improve environmental sanitation
- Identify and promote alternative sources of energy and technology
- Institutionalize capacity building in rural communities

To accomplish the above objectives, the National Youth Service Corps (NYSC) designed a three-phase program. The first, "Operation Rollback the Sahara," was launched in Northern Nigeria in July 1966, and the second, "Operation Soil Integrity," was initiated in the South in August of the same year. The second phase was the establishment of two or more "Eco-Plazas" in each state, which depending on need, viability, and available finance, would increase the number with time. An Eco-Plaza is a multipurpose complex that has residential quarters for corps members as well as rooms for meetings, workshops, clinics, office space, and other activities. Phase three would focus on intensive agricultural development, development of agro-allied industries, and the application of appropriate technologies to enable citizens and their communities in rural areas meet their needs and achieve self-sufficiency.

A few years after this program was conceptualized, one of the authors of this book (Ukaga) became involved in it as a consultant and a director of an Institute at Colorado State University that signed a Memorandum of Understanding to work together with the NYSC on this project. By this time, the above program objectives and plan of action have already been developed, mainly by top NYSC officials with little input or participation by other stakeholders, such as the field staff and "youth corpers," who would play a major role in implementing the program, or local communities and citizens that these programs were supposed to benefit.

It was apparent that the top officials of the NYSC were solely in control of the program. They determined the agenda, process, objectives, and action plan. Only a few relatively homogenous, primary stakeholders were invited to participate in planning the program. Local citizens had neither meaningful decision-making authority nor were actively involved in all aspects of planning and implementing the program.

Ukaga was therefore pleased when the director of the Integrated Rural Development Program and three other officials of the Nigerian National Youth Service Corps attended a two-week workshop on "participatory processes for sustainable development." The workshop was designed to help participants gain appreciation for and skills in using participatory approaches to plan and implement sustainable development programs from the bottom-up. As you might imagine, this enhanced the participants' interest in participatory program planning and their personal ability to do so. It also helped aforementioned officials partially overcome the effects of their formal authoritarian education and professional experience by teaching them to use participatory methods.

When Ukaga visited Nigeria a few years later, with colleagues from Colorado State University, they found that the workshop had influenced some "practice change" in the officials from the Nigerian National Youth Service Corps. It was obvious that these officials became more engaged in participatory methods of community development than they were prior to attending the workshop. However, it was also obvious that, once these officials returned to work and tried to plan projects in a participatory fashion, they found themselves sliding back to their usual top-down mode of operation due to structural constraints on the one hand and habit on the other, which shows that it takes more than a single effort, like the workshop, to assure participation.

Assuring participation takes time, interest, skill, hard work, and planning, as well as constant effort. It simply does not happen by accident. It is therefore advisable to guarantee, as much as humanly possible, the meaningful participation of all legitimate interested parties by making sure that:

- The various interests and segments of the target population are represented among participating citizens.

- All legitimate parties participate meaningfully in decision making. For instance, it is imperative in the evaluation of sustainable development that citizens determine for themselves the questions to be asked and the results to be obtained.

- Participants have equitable voices in program planning and implementation, regardless of their socio-economic status or other characteristics. This means: (a) recognizing that people would come in with existing disparities in power, roles, interests, and so on, and (b) taking steps (such as paying attention to persons who are relatively less powerful) to mitigate negative consequences of such disparities.

- Assure that every project activity is participant-oriented.

- Participants develop and/or use customized approaches to evaluation and tools that are effective and manageable for what they need to accomplish.

- Citizens develop evaluation skills that would be useful in their projects.

- Trust is built among participants so that they can cooperatively plan and implement necessary activities as a group.

Finally, it is important to note that, while participation tends to take more time in the beginning (is "front-end loaded," as it were) compared to the top-down approach, the extra time spent in the beginning to assure active citizen participation is usually more than compensated for by the time NOT spent fighting for acceptance, agreement, ownership, and implementation of the plan at the "back end" of the process. Patience and skillful facilitation is needed to nurture the spirit and practice of participation.[61] While one person can decide in the twinkling of an eye what to do, it usually takes more time and effort to get a group of diverse individuals to settle on a plan or course of action. Nevertheless, skilled facilitators can make it easier for all participants to work cooperatively by evoking participation; promoting a safe, interactive environment; unleashing people's enthusiasm; and encouraging creativity through stimulating discussions, games, and other group facilitation techniques.

Involving People

Although we have stated it several times, we cannot overemphasize that a vitally important component of evaluating sustainable development is local citizen participation in planning, implementing, and monitoring programs, policies, and projects. The goal is to improve the quality of popular participation instead of merely its quantity.

Evaluating sustainability is based on the assumption that the best ideas usually come from the people, not the policymakers. Therefore, active participation is necessary to direct the evaluation process, which exposes citizens to the ramifications of their thoughts and actions on others, their local environment, and the surrounding landscape, as well as motivating and organizing people to direct change within the context of a shared vision for their collective future. Its aim is for citizens to control the evaluation process through their ideas and information, which, as part of the process, are self-empowering.

People want the most effective development *and* evaluation process possible, one that is honestly used through participation in a truly democratic way. Participative development must begin with a firm belief in the potential of people. It arises both out of a leader's heart and his or her personal commitment to people and out of the heart of the democratic principle: the right to an open, accessible process; the right and duty to influence decision making; the right and duty to understand the results; and the duty to be accountable for those results.

To accomplish a participative evaluation, leaders must create and maintain emotionally safe environments within which people can develop quality relationships with one another. Creating such an environment requires at least six things:

- Respect for one another
- Understanding and accepting that what people believe precedes policy and practice
- Agreement on the rights of participation in and access to the entire evaluation process from its inception to the outcome of its results
- Understanding that most people work as volunteers and need personal covenants, not legal contracts
- Understanding that relationships count more than structure because people—not structures—build trust

- Protecting the process against capture by self-serving financial and political interests

The needs of the various committee's are best met by meeting the needs of its individuals. If this is done, evaluating sustainability can be productive, rewarding, meaningful, maturing, enriching, fulfilling, healing, and joyful. Participative development is one of the greatest privileges in our democracy, and the participative evaluation of development is one of our greatest responsibilities.

Nevertheless, a creative evaluation is difficult to handle because in such a process almost everyone, at different times and in various ways, plays four roles: one as creator, another as implementer, a third as temporary leader with a specific expertise demanded by a given circumstance, and finally as follower, supporter, and helper.

Although implementation of an evaluation is often as creative as the questions to which it is responding, it is at this very point that leaders and managers may find it most difficult to be open to the influence of others. Nevertheless, by conceiving a shared vision and pursuing it together, a local community's problems of cultural adaptability and their evaluation can be resolved, and the community members may simultaneously and fundamentally alter their concept of adaptability, sustainability, development, and evaluation. But this requires "joint ownership" of the entire process.

The heart of sustainability is joint ownership of the process for each person involved. Because owners cannot walk away from their concerns, everyone's accountability begins to change. Ownership demands increasing maturity on everyone's part, which is probably best expressed in a continually rising level of literacy: participative literacy, ownership literacy, evaluation literacy, sustainable development literacy, and so on. And ownership demands a commitment to be as informed as possible about the whole.

Joint ownership is an intimate, personal experience in that each person commits himself or herself to both the process *and* its outcome. One's beliefs are connected to the intimacy of one's experience and come before and have primacy over policies, standards, or practices. This intimate, personal commitment to the evaluation process affects one's accountability and draws out one's personal authenticity.

No evaluation process can amount to anything without the people who make it what it is. It is initially what the people are and finally what the people become. People do not grow by knowing all the answers; they grow by living with the questions and their possibilities. The art of working together thus lies in how people deal with change, how they deal with conflict, and how they reach their potential.

The intimacy of ownership arises from translating personal and community values into a plan for a sustainable future through an evaluation of what is needed to create that future. The intimacy of ownership seeks its excellence in a search for truth, wisdom, justice, and knowledge—all tempered with intuition, compassion, and mercy. The people of a community must therefore make a covenant, a promise with one another: to honor and protect the sacred nature of their relationships so that each may reflect unity, grace, poise, creativity, and justice. If they base decisions on the intrinsic value of human diversity, and if they base decisions on the notion that every person brings a unique offering to the evaluation process, then inclusivity will be the only path open to them.

Including people—really including people—in the evaluation process means helping them to understand the process, their place within it, and their accountability for the outcome. It means giving others the chance to do their best according to the diversity of their gifts, which is fundamental to the equality that environmental justice requires and democracy inspires. Finally, a community must be committed to using wisely and responsibly its environment and its finite resources, which means a conscious, sustainable, reciprocal relationship between the local community and its surrounding landscape—beginning with an evaluation of what is necessary for sustainable development.

To create the desired change, however, it is essential that all affected groups in the community be involved in the process and trained in the skills of leadership. It is further necessary that the people responsible for a local program, policy, or project be involved in its evaluation, creation, and monitoring to increase the probability of a successful outcome. If not, a political problem arises because evaluating sustainable community development is initially site specific, and that, in our experience, inevitably brings up either turf struggles or a blatant denial of both responsibility and accountability by passing the buck.

One of us (Maser) spent over two years on a citizens committee to advise his home county on environmental issues. During that time, the city and county did not coordinate between the city and its surrounding landscape, especially with respect to water for the future. In turn, when things got uncomfortable, the county insisted that it did not have the jurisdiction and therefore neither the responsibility nor accountability. Those belonged to the state because the land-use plan had been carried out at the state level.

Such top-down planning does not work because communities have no vested interest in doing what they feel will benefit someone else. Thus, little gets done with sufficient forethought to be of real long-term social-environmental benefit to the future. As long as the majority of the people in a community, county, state, or nation are predominantly self-centered, and thus myopic, each and every level of government must see a clear—and often immediately personal—advantage before cooperation and coordination become a reality. This is important, because to cooperate and coordinate implies the willing acceptance of both responsibility and accountability, which most people seem to avoid whenever possible.

Culture and Sustainability

Living culture is embodied in the people themselves, and it is there one must search for an understanding of the people as a whole. In this sense, each person is both the creator and the keeper of a unique piece of the cultural tapestry, an understanding of which one can glean only by seeing it simultaneously from many points of view, much as an insect sees.

Our perceptions can be thought of as similar to an insect's compound eyes because it is through perception that we "see" one another and everything else. An insect's compound eyes are formed from a group of separate visual elements, each of which corresponds to a single facet of the eye's outer surface, which may vary from a few hundred to a few thousand facets, depending on the kind of insect. Each facet has in turn what amounts to a single nerve fiber that sends optical messages to the brain. Seeing with an insect's compound eyes would be like seeing with many different eyes, with many different perceptions simultaneously.

Each perception of a component of one's community is like a facet in the compound eye of an insect, with its independent nerve fiber connecting it to the local community and hence expanding outward to the regional, national, and global society (the various levels of our increasingly collective and abstract brain). Thus, each perception, composed of many elements, including an individual's personal and cultural foundation, has its unique construct. This of course establishes the limits of an individual's understanding.

A person who tends to be positive or optimistic, for example, sees a glass of water as half full, while a person who tends to be negative or pessimistic sees the same glass of water as half empty. Regardless of the way it is perceived, the level of water is the same, which illustrates that we see what we choose to see, which has everything to do with perception but may have little to do with reality.

The important implication is that the freer people are as individuals to change their perceptions without social resistance in the form of ridicule or shame, the freer is a community (the collection of individual perceptions) to adapt to change in a healthy developmental or evolutionary way. On the other hand, the more people are ridiculed or shamed into accepting the politically correct ideas of others, the more prone a community is to the cracking of its moral foundation and to the crumbling of its social infrastructure, because social change cannot long be held in abeyance, which poses questions to which one must respond. As Sam Goldwyn once said, "For your information, let me ask you a few questions."

Before the people of a community are ready to evaluate the sustainability of their future, they must ask and answer two questions: (1) Who are we today as a culture? (2) What legacy do we want to leave our children? These questions are critical because the notion of "legacy," which every culture understands as a notion of the heart, can be used in place of "sustainability," which is a formalized Western notion of the intellect.

Who Are We as a Culture?

Who are we culturally—now, today? This is a difficult but necessary question for people to deal with because evaluating sustainability is the palpable nexus between a fading memory of the past and the anticipation of an uncertain future. The people of a community must therefore decide, based on how they define their present cultural identity, what kind of evaluation to create. A people's self-held concept (individual, cultural, and universal values) is critical to their cultural future because their personal and cultural self-image will determine what their community will become socially, which in turn will determine what their children will become socially.

The question of who we are culturally may be a more important question today than it would have been in the recent past because there are times in history, such as today, when two eras run parallel to each other, when one is dying while the other is struggling with its infancy. This can be a deeply disturbing, confusing, and divisive time as different world views, cultural patterns and assumptions, and predominant means of livelihood compete with one another in an effort to give meaning and direction to life.

Such a time of raw chaos and naked transition can be terribly frightening and thus lead people to retreat into the simplistic solutions often associated with fundamentalism. Fundamentalism (which can ensnare both the political right and left or the spiritual and secular) is characterized by a rigid, impervious belief system that relentlessly widens the polarity between the safe "us" and the dangerous "them." Because it is founded in fear (which is always divisive) and becomes the embodiment of fear that feeds on itself, fundamentalism is not only incapable of tolerating diverse views and backgrounds but also far less capable of creatively asking new questions and discovering new answers within a context of dynamic complexity.

Fundamentalism, which is so prevalent in today's political discourse, is simply not up to the challenge of our times. Instead, the next stage of cultural evolution must focus inward, into each person's consciousness, because this is the only realm out of which can grow creative, self-organizing innovations that offer sustainable ways of living, which are, after all, based on the quality of both interpersonal relationships and those between humanity and its environment.

Cultural evolution, like all evolution, thrives in a context rich in diversity and complexity, wherein myriad opportunities for interaction exist. Self-organizing innovations can emerge out of such a setting as people search for ways to live consciously and sustainably in every sense of the word. These innovations become "attractors," which draw people out of the chaotic soup into further experimentation with social-environmental sustainability.

The most powerful attractors are those that respond to people's basic requirements for survival and to their deepest yearnings for such things as connection, meaning, and transcendence, all of which add up to personal wholeness. When these attractors resonate among large numbers of people (a critical mass), society shifts, but people must first be aware of these "attractors" amid the flotsam and jetsam of change in which the decay of the dying era seems, at least momentarily, to overwhelm the formative one.

Of course, there initially is a multitude who, preferring the devil they know to the devil they don't, steadfastly swear allegiance to the passing era by clinging tenaciously to old views and old ways of doing things. But there is also an expanding group of "younger" people who find the present and future ripe with possibilities. And it is here, in the present, that small choices and actions can have major, albeit unpredictable, effects in determining what comes next and how it manifests.

And somewhere among the millions of choices and thousands of experiments with conscious living is the possibility that they will coalesce into a renewed community endowed life with real meaning. For such a community to be viable, however, it would have to be anchored on the bedrock value of social-environmental sustainability in all its various aspects.

Thomas Jefferson gave good counsel on values: "In matters of principle, stand like a rock. In matters of taste, swim with the current." To identify those principles and/or values on which one stands firm, one can ask: What are the fundamental principles that I believe in to the point of no compromise? What values are central to my being?

Categories of Value

The Ch'an masters who carried Zen to Japan brought Confucian ethics with them. In discussing these fundamental values as a guide to personal behavior, Confucius said, "If a man will carefully cultivate these in his conduct, he may still err a little, but he won't be far from the standard of truth." When we as individuals clearly understand and can explicitly articulate our personal values, then we can live in keeping with them.

Let's consider three categories of values: universal, cultural, and individual. Universal (or archetypal) values reveal to people the human condition and inform them of their place within it.[62] Through universal values, one connects one's individual experiences with the rest of humanity (the collective unconscious) and the cosmos. Here, the barriers of time and place, of language and culture disappear in the ever-changing dance of life. Universal values must be experienced; they cannot be comprehended. Can you, for example, know a sunset? Fathom a drop of water? Translate a smile? Define love?

Universal values are the timeless constants brought to different cultures at various times throughout history. Just as the hub remains ever still as the wheel revolves, so universal values remain ever the center of human life, no matter where the wheel travels—from the past into present and from the present toward the future. These are the truths of the human condition toward which people aspire (such as joy, unity, love, and peace); of these the sages have spoken in many tongues.

Cultural (or ethnic) values are those of the day and are socially agreed upon. They are established to create and maintain social order in a particular time and place and can be highly volatile. Cultural values concern ethics and human notions of right and wrong, good or evil, in terms of customs and manners.

In culture one sees reflected the ideas and behaviors of a society that rewards or punishes according to the perceived alignment of an individual member to its values. Hence, cultural values can be a "mixed bag" for an individual, especially in a highly complex society that is rapidly losing its sense of family, community, and mythology, like that of the United States or Japan, where there is much that may resonate with an individual and much that may not.

Every culture is a person in a sense, and like people, there is the potential for creative interaction and/or conflict when cultures meet. Although people in the world today are all too familiar with cultural conflicts and the destruction they have wrought, it is well to remember that a meeting of cultures also triggers tremendous explosions of creativity in such things as language, ethics, education, law, philosophy, and government.

Individual (or personal) values are constituted by the private meanings people bestow on those concepts and experiences (such as marriage vows or spiritual teachings) that are personally important. These meanings are in large part a result of how people are raised by their families of origin and what of their parents' values they take with them in the form of personal temperament. These meanings may change, however, depending on one's experiences in life and how much one is willing to grow psychologically and spiritually as a result of those experiences. As such, individual values are reflected in such things as personal goals, humor, relationships, and commitments.

Thus, how well people's core values are encompassed in the design of an evaluation of their notion of sustainability depends first on how well the people understand themselves individually and as a culture, which means how well they understand their core values, and second on how well that understanding is reflected on paper, where there can be no question about what has been stated and how. Let's consider the First Canadians with whom Maser has worked.

The First Canadians have departed from their old culture because they have, against their will, been forced to adopt European-Canadian ways, which means they have given up or lost their ancestral ways. Yet they have not, by choice, totally adopted white culture and want to retain some degree of their ancestral culture. Thus, the three questions they must ask and answer are: Which of our ancestral ways still have sufficient cultural value for us to keep them? Which of the white ways do we want to or are we willing to adopt? How do we put the chosen elements of both cultures together in such a way that we can today define who we are culturally?

For example, in 1993, Maser was asked to review an ecological brief for a First Nation in western British Columbia, Canada, whose reservation is located between the sea and land immediately down slope from that which a timber company wanted to cut. The problem lay in the fact that the timber company could only reach the timber it wanted to cut by obtaining an easement through the reservation, which gave the First Nation some control over the timber company. The First Nation wanted this control to have an active voice in how the timber company would log the upper-slope forest, because the outcome would for many years affect the reservation with respect to The First Nation's sense of place and social-environmental sustainability.

By virtue of the company's required easement through the First Nation's land, the First Nation was the strong organizing context that would control the behavior of the timber company as it logged the upper-slope forest. If, however, the timber company had not been required to pass through the First Nation's land, it could, through self-serving logging practices, easily have become the uncontrollable cancer that would have destroyed the cultural values of the First Nation's land for many generations.

Before meeting with the timber company, the First Nation's chief asked for some counsel. Maser's reply was as follows:

> Before I discuss the ecological brief I've been asked to review, there are three points that must be taken into account if what I say is to have any value to the First Nation. What I'm about to say may be difficult to hear, but I say it with the utmost respect.
>
> Point 1: Who are you, the First Nation, in a cultural sense? You are not your old culture because you have—against your will—been forced to adopt some white ways, which means you have given up or lost a lot of your ancestral ways. You are not—by choice—white, so you may wish to retain some of your ancestral ways. The questions you must ask and answer are the following: What of our ancestral ways still have sufficient value that we want to keep them? What of the white ways do we want to or are we willing to adopt? How do we put the chosen elements of both cultures together in such a way that we can today define who we are as a culture?

Point 2: What do you want your children to have as a legacy from your decisions and your negotiations with the timber company? Whatever you decide is what you are committing your children, their children, and their children's children to pay as the effects of your decisions unto the seventh generation and beyond. This, of course, is solely your choice and that is as it should be. I make no judgments. But whatever you choose will partly answer Point 3.

Point 3: What do you want your reservation to look like and act like during and after logging by the timber company? How you define yourselves culturally, what choices you make for your children, and the conscious decisions you make about the condition of your land will determine what you end up with. In all of these things, the choice is yours. The consequences belong to both you and your children.

What about you, the reader? Who are you today? We each change personally as we grow in years and experience. So do our respective communities. Each community that wishes to conduct an evaluation in order to promote a sustainable future must therefore ask of itself: Who are we today in a cultural sense? Then, based on how a community sees itself, each community must ask: Who do we want to be or to become in the future? These are important questions and must be clearly answered on paper for all to see, because how they are answered will determine the nonnegotiable constraints that set the overall direction of a community's vision and thus the legacy inherited by its children. To answer who we are as a community today and what we want as a community in the future, it is advantageous to begin by honestly evaluating your own set of values.

Identifying Values to Safeguard

Although it may not seem important at any particular moment in a given day, it is critical in the long run to know what values to safeguard in one's community. After all, values shape the contours of people's lives. For example, a simple act by the very people who went to Phoenix, Arizona, to find relief from their allergies has placed Arizona among the top ten percent of states in pollen count during the six-week allergy season.[63]

Before urban sprawl began consuming the desert, the area around Phoenix was a haven for people who suffered from allergies. Doctors in the 1940s and 1950s sent patients there because the dry air was virtually pollen-free. But many of those people also brought with them their nondesert plants, which subsequently matured and now fill the air with pollen during the spring of each year.

In addition, the dry climate causes pollen grains from non-indigenous plants to stay aloft and ride the air currents, wafting in every zephyr. They are not washed from dry desert air, as they are in nondesert areas that experience spring rains. So the allergy sufferers themselves made their own haven into their worst nightmare by not identifying and protecting the very value that brought them to Phoenix, Arizona, in the first place—air virtually free of pollen.

With the above in mind, you would be wise to pause for a moment and describe to yourself how you feel about your community before you begin to craft your evaluation of sustainability. What types of images come to mind? Who do you think about in your community and why? What places do you think about (open space, shopping malls, schools)? Do activities present themselves? If so, which ones? In short, characterize your community, and be sure to do so either by recording your questions and answers on tape or by putting them in writing.

If you find that you are unsure how you feel about something, take the time to consciously observe your community; see how it functions and how you feel about the way it functions. How friendly is it? How safe do you feel living and moving about in it during the day and at night?

If you are still not sure you have covered all the bases, put yourself in the position of a consultant who has been hired to characterize your community. What questions would you, as a consultant, ask the residents? Why did you select these particular questions? What are you hoping they will tell you? Why do you think these particular questions are important? Now continue your observations and answer the questions for yourself.

Based on what you see and feel, what values do you hold that are met in your community and why? Which values are not met and why?

By asking these question of oneself, it becomes clear that framing good questions is the key to crafting an evaluation. Now, using this technique, characterize and design the community of your dreams. What would it be like? Can you see where, how, and why your interests and talents would fit into your vision? Describe in writing its primary elements, remembering that the most important part of community, by the very nature of the concept, revolves around the quality of human relationships and the reciprocal partnership between the community and its landscape.

If even a small group of community members is willing to participate in such a personalized exercise, it would quickly become apparent that the makings of a sound evaluation of sustainable development are contained in the collective of the personal observations, feelings, and values. But taken alone, personal values are not enough. The pulse of the community as a whole must also be taken.

Ferreting Out Community Values

To ask a relevant question about where you are going, you must know not only where you want to go but also where you are, which means taking stock of *who* you are. Whereas a shared vision is a statement of where you want your community to go, evaluating your community, including the reciprocity of its relationship to the immediate landscape, as it is today allows you to determine your starting point for the journey and what you need to do along the way.

One way of assessing a community is by entering into its routines. This means selecting people to attend school events, visiting people in their kitchens and living rooms, and going into cafes, gas stations, laundromats, marketplaces, and other places where people gather, such as taverns and houses of worship (for example, churches, temples, and mosques). The purpose of these visits is to interact with residents to determine such things as what they do for work and what their work routines are, their personal interests, recreational patterns, what support services are important to them, and how they feel about changes within the community and between the community and its landscape.

To really understand how a community sees itself, one must ask people not only what they like about their community and its landscape and why but also what they do not like and why. One must ask people what they most want to change about their community and its landscape. Questions also help one find out which informal networks people use both to communicate with one another and to solve problems, as well as who they trust and rely on as communicators and caretakers.

Alternatively, a consultant can be hired to design the questions and derive the answers by visiting personally and informally with community members in both their places of business and their homes. Here the watchword is *trust*. The people *must* *trust* the consultant(s), because people do not care how much a person knows until they first know how much that person genuinely cares about them.

It is, after all, the quality and sustainability of one's own community that are being mapped into the future, and that is no small matter. It is thus important to understand that trust is heightened and the community's purpose is served to the extent that members of the community become actively engaged in the process.

The purpose of asking such questions is to make the informal system of community clearly visible in such a way that by understanding the range of issues people are concerned about and how they see themselves in relationship to those issues, one can help the community recognize and express its current cultural identity. This kind of information is called ethnography in anthropology, or "the story of the people."

The story of the people as a baseline description of how the people identify themselves culturally is a sound preparatory step toward crafting an evaluation of community sustainability. This process of interaction within a community at the informal level has two important effects.

One, it fosters empowerment of the people themselves and as a community because personal and social reflection not only determines the intelligence and possible consequences of any given action but also leads citizens to see what the next step might be and to take it. It is thus important, as French philosopher Henri Bergson observed, to "think like a man [person] of action, and act like a man [person] of thought."

Two, it can prompt social institutions into becoming more responsive because people within agencies gain insight into the concerns of citizens and thus into a community's cultural identity by participating in the ongoing "story of the people." Such participation gives agency people good and relevant information that makes sense to the citizens and allows them to understand why citizens say what they do. This notion is reminiscent of a statement made by Mahatma Gandhi to an audience of India's bureaucrats and social elite: "Until we stand in the hot sun with the millions that toil every day in the fields, we will not speak for them."

In this statement, Gandhi showed that he understood the basis of real public opinion, which ranges from a vague general feeling to a specific set of beliefs for which people are willing to die. Public opinion is characterized as much by emotions as by logic and is determined by self-interest, which, with your help, can be expanded from a strictly individualistic, self-centered self-interest into an "enlightened" (more conscious), broader (community) self-interest.

One important fact must be kept in mind, however; information alone will rarely change the ideas and opinions held by people, especially if the information is in a purely abstract form. Good public relations works more on the "hidden" levels of thought and feelings, those exemplified by the trust embodied in genuine mutual goodwill, as opposed to the level of logic that is purely intellectual.

Gandhi, by insisting on meeting the downtrodden masses of India on their own ground, established the credibility and genuineness of his understanding of their plight and of his love for them, and this made all the difference because they felt not only that they knew him but also that they could trust him. And trust is the key to one's belief in and willingness to follow the lead of another person.

One of the ways Gandhi garnered the people's trust was to deal fairly with all sides (including the British, regardless of their behavior), which is critical because in almost any subject there is controversy when viewed from more than one perspective. This means that one must guard carefully against arrogance in one's own point of view and one's behavior because arrogance will almost always cause the listeners to resent whatever is being said, no matter how well founded it may be.

Consider that in today's world, the intangible asset of "goodwill," which is analogous to trust, is rated surprisingly high in value as part of the total price of purchasing a business. Building the intangible asset of goodwill takes many years of diligent, consistent effort; once earned, few organizations are willing to relinquish it. Individuals, such as community leaders (and evaluators), not only can but also must build this asset over time if they are to be effective.

Earning the trust and goodwill of one's fellow citizens is critical today because, having been lied to so often by experts, people are more skeptical than ever before and thus reluctant to place their trust in people they do not personally know. Even then, they may be cautious. Nothing persuades an audience to examine your point of view as much as personal trust. This said, the conclusions to which your evaluation and presentation may bring an audience is only useful if there is a powerful drive to act in accord with those conclusions.

Whether one likes it or not, what usually motivates people is their own self-interest. With this in mind, experience shows that a persuasive message is more likely to be accepted and acted upon if it meets the following criteria:

- It provides for a personal necessity or desire ("If you do this, it will protect your quality of life.")

- It is in harmony with group beliefs ("We all know that social-environmental sustainability is . . .")

- The audience is led to the final conclusion and then left to discover it for themselves ("Based on past experience and current knowledge, it seems self-evident that . . .")

Whatever method is used to gather the information, it must be based on personal trust and goodwill, in addition to which the people must ultimately craft the evaluation themselves, possibly with the help of a neutral third-party facilitator, which brings us to a community's legacy.

What Legacy Do We Want to Leave Our Children?

Once a group of people, whether a community has defined itself culturally (present and future), it can decide what legacy it wants to leave its children. This must be done consciously, however, because the consequences of whatever decisions the group makes under its "new cultural" identity are what the group is committing its children, their children, and their children's children to pay.

The rest of Maser's reply to The First Nation in Canada applies here:

> Now to my comments: This is a difficult task at best. As with any definition, it is a human invention and has no meaning to Nature. Therefore, you must tell the timber company, clearly

and concisely, what the terms in this ecological brief mean to you and how you interpret them with respect to the company's actions that will affect your reservation.

1. Every ecosystem functions fully within the limits (constraints) imposed on it by Nature and/or humans. Therefore, it is the type, scale, and duration of the alterations to the system—the imposed limits—that you need to be concerned with.

   If your reservation looks the way you want it to and functions the way you want it to, then the question becomes: How must we and the timber company behave to keep it looking and functioning the way it is? If, on the other hand, your reservation does not look the way you want it to and does not function the way you want it to, then the question becomes: How must we and the timber company behave to make it look and function the way we want it to?

   But regardless of your decisions or the company's actions, your reservation will always function to its greatest capacity under the circumstances (constraints) Nature, you, and the company impose on it. The point is that your decisions and the company's actions, excluding what Nature may do, will determine how your reservation both looks and functions. This reflects the importance of the preceding Point 3, which is: what you want your reservation to look like and how you want it to function *after* the timber company has left. It also reflects the importance of what you decide.

2. If you want the landscape of your reservation to look and function in a certain way, then how must the timber company's landscape look and function to help make your reservation be what you want it to be? Keep in mind that the landscape of your reservation and the company's timber holdings are both made up of the collective performance of individual stands of trees or "habitat patches" (a stand is a human-delineated group of standing trees). Therefore, how the stands look and function will

determine how the collective landscape looks and functions.

3. Remember that any undesirable ecological effects are also undesirable economic effects over time. Your interest in your reservation will be there for many, many years, generations perhaps, but the company's interest in the forest may well disappear just as soon as the trees are cut. So, the company's short-term economic decision may be good for them immediately but may at the same time be a bad long-term ecological and thus a bad long-term economic decision for you.

4. To maintain ecological functions means that you must maintain the characteristics of the ecosystem in such a way that its processes are sustainable. The characteristics you must be concerned about are: (1) composition, (2) structure, (3) function, and (4) Nature's disturbance regimes, which periodically alter the ecosystem's composition, structure, and function.

   The composition or kinds of plants and their age classes within a plant community create a certain structure that is characteristic of the plant community at any given age. It is the structure of the plant community that in turn creates and maintains certain functions. In addition, it is the composition, structure, and function of a plant community that determine what kinds of animals can live there, how many, and for how long. If you change the composition of the plant community, you change the structure, hence the function, and you affect the animals. People and Nature are continually changing a community's structure by altering its composition, which in turn affects how it functions.

   For example, the timber company wants to change the forest's structure by cutting the trees, which in turn will change the plant community's composition, which in turn will change how the community functions, which in turn will change the kinds and numbers of animals that can live there. These are the key elements with which you

must be concerned, because an effect on one area can—
and usually does—affect the entire landscape.

Composition, structure, and function go together to
create and maintain ecological processes both in time and
across space, and it is the health of the processes that in
the end creates the forest. Your forest is a living organism,
not just a collection of trees—as the timber industry
usually thinks of it.

5. Scale is an often-forgotten component of healthy forests
and landscapes. The treatment of every stand of timber is
critically important to the health of the whole landscape,
which is a collection of the interrelated stands.

Thus, when you deal only with a stand, you are
ignoring the relationship of that particular stand to other
stands, to the rest of the drainage, and to the landscape.
It's like a jigsaw puzzle where each piece is a stand. The
relationship of certain pieces (stands) makes a picture
(drainage). The relationship of the pictures (drainages)
makes a whole puzzle (landscape). Thus, relationships of
all the stands within a particular area make a drainage
and the relationships of all the drainages within a
particular area make the landscape.

If one piece is left out of the puzzle, it is not complete.
If one critical piece is missing, it may be very difficult to
figure out what the picture is. So each piece (stand) is
critically important in its relationship to the completion of
the whole puzzle (landscape). Therefore, the way each
stand is defined and treated by the timber company is
critically important to how the landscape, encompassing
both the company's land and your reservation, looks and
functions over time.

6. Degrading an ecosystem is a human concept based on
human values and has nothing to do with Nature. Nature
places no extrinsic value on anything. Everything just is,
and in its being it is perfect (intrinsic value). Therefore,
when considering intrinsic value, if something in Nature
changes, it simply changes—no value is either added or

subtracted. But superimposing the extrinsic value of human desires on Nature's intrinsic value creates a different proposition. Thus, whether or not your reservation becomes degraded depends on what you want it to be like, what value or values you have placed on its being in a certain condition, to produce certain things for you. If your desired condition is negatively affected by the company's actions, then your reservation becomes degraded. If your desired condition is positively affected by the company's actions, then your reservation is improved. Remember, your own actions can also degrade or improve your reservation.

7. It is important that you know—as clearly as possible—what the definitions in this brief really mean to you and your choices for your children and your reservation. Only when you fully understand what these definitions mean to you can you negotiate successfully with the timber company.

We hope the foregoing gives you, the reader, an idea of how to approach other cultures and help them design their own evaluations of community sustainability based on asking questions that allow them to define "sustainability" for themselves through their answers to the questions they learn to ask.

Balancing Thoroughness with Political "Reality"

One of the major challenges in conducting any evaluation is the difficult task of balancing the need for thoroughness with the need to be responsive to political "reality," however that is defined. Trying to simultaneously maximize technical quality and responsiveness is difficult at best. The more attention paid to scientific rigor rather than political considerations in an evaluation, the more valid and reliable results may be, but at the risk of rendering the evaluation nonviable. Conversely, the more attention paid to citizen concerns and political considerations rather than scientific rigor, the more politically viable the project may be although this viability is probably "purchased" at the expense of the scientific validity, reliability, and generalizability of the results.

The goal, then, is to synchronize both variables (political reality and scientific rigor) in such a way that neither the technical quality of the evaluation nor its responsiveness to prevailing political "realities" is significantly compromised. In other words, citizens involved in evaluation of sustainable development politics should not let politics jeopardize the scientific rigor and integrity of the evaluation, and at the same time they should not pursue scientific rigor like puritans or horses with blinders on by omitting the consideration of political realities.

A good way to achieve this goal is through an iterative, participatory planning processes in which all factors (political, scientific, methodological, financial, cultural, logistic, and so on) are fully discussed and considered in designing a customized evaluation plan for the project at hand.

You, the reader, may recall that the above strategy (to balance the need for thoroughness with the need for responsiveness to political reality) was used in the Colorado evaluation project discussed earlier in this book. In that case, stakeholders determined the questions to ask, developed the instruments for data collection, and selected research designs for the evaluation project by using a participatory planning process that was both iterative and participatory. The observations, concerns, and suggestions of various stakeholders were compiled and used to guide project planning and implementation. This process provided adequate opportunity for citizens to identify, discuss, and address important factors that they believed should be considered in designing the evaluation.

The purpose of the evaluation was to determine if and how abstinence education projects being implemented across the State of Colorado were successful in enabling participating youth to abstain from sexual activity. One issue in evaluating of the Colorado abstinence education project that highlighted the challenge of balancing the need for thoroughness with being responsive to political reality had to do with the type of questions respondents could be asked.

From the perspective of scientific rigor, it was necessary that participants be asked questions, such as "Have you ever had sex before?" and "When was the last time you had sex?" in order to determine if the abstinence education was effective. Knowing if and how participants' sexual behavior differed before, during, and after the abstinence education would help evaluators determine what (if any) difference the program had made.

From an ethical and political perspective, there was concern that such questions might not be appropriate for the target population (preadolescents and adolescents). Specifically, there was a justified concern that sexually explicit questions were not appropriate for this age group, and that such questions would make it difficult (if not impossible) to get permission from parents and/or guardians, schools, and school boards to conduct the evaluation.

There was thus tension between the need to ask participants questions that would reveal if (and how) the abstinence education program made any difference in their sexual behavior and the need to avoid asking participants questions that may be seen as inappropriate. Based on the above considerations, the interested parties decided to produce two versions of the instruments. It was agreed that one version, with no explicit questions about sexual activity, would be for younger participants (preadolescents), while another version for older participants (adolescents) would have such questions, but the questions must be appropriately phrased.

Through an iterative process of developing, critiquing, and improving several drafts of the instruments for data collection, the stakeholders finally produced instruments they all agreed had responded to political and socio-cultural concerns without compromising the scientific rigor or general effectiveness of the evaluation. The instruments eventually produced and adopted by the group through this iterative, participatory process included items that elicited demographic data, information about school achievement, substance abuse, home environment, self-efficacy, and attitudes toward premarital sexual intercourse. Input from African American and Hispanic citizens assured that questions were culturally appropriate. Further, the instrument was translated into Spanish based on feedback from Hispanic participants during pretests so that Hispanic respondents who prefer to use the Spanish version of these instruments could do so.[64]

Conclusion

There are many voices when dealing with sustainable development and its evaluation. It is wise, therefore, to remember that success or failure is not an event, but rather the interpretation of an event. And who interprets an event's outcome is critical because one person may think the event was a wonderful success and another may think it was a dismal failure. Those who can best judge the success or failure of a project designed and implemented to achieve sustainable development are those who participated fully in all aspects of the project, including its evaluation. With this note, we wish you every possible success in achieving the sustainable development you are striving for.

ENDNOTES

1. World Council on Environment and Development, *Our Common Future* (New York: Oxford University Press, 1987).
2. Michael Redclift, *Sustainable Development: Exploring the Contradictions* (London: Methuen Press, 1987).
3. See endnote 1 above.
4. Geoffrey Nwaka, "Planning Sustainable Cities in Africa," *Canadian Journal of Urban Research* 5 no. 1 (June 1996): 119–136. See also C. Bartone, "Environmental Challenges in the Third World Cities," *Journal of the American Planning Association* 4 no. 54 (1992): 411–415; and J. E. Hardoy and D. Satterwaite, *Environmental Problems in Third World Cities: An Agenda for the Poor and the Planet* (London: IIED, 1992).
5. Wilfred Berkerman, *Green Colored Glasses: Environmentalism Reconsidered* (Washington D.C.: CATO Institute, 1996).
6. Sophie Poklewski Koziell, "Two Women of the Soil," *Resurgence* 195 (1999): 36–38.
7. Chris Maser, *Vision and Leadership in Sustainable Development* (Boca Raton, FL.: Lewis Publishers, 1998).
8. See endnote 7 above.
9. See Brian M. Stecher and W. Alan Davis, *How to Focus an Evaluation* (Newsbury Park, CA.: Sage Publications, 1978).
10. Michael Redclift, "Reflections on the 'Sustainable Development Debate,'" *International Journal of Sustainable Development and World Ecology* 1 (1994): 3–21.
11. Our discussion of the approaches to defining sustainability and developing indicators is based in part on John L. Warren, *How Do We Know What Is Sustainable? A Retrospective and Prospective View.* In *Principles of Sustainable Development.* Edited by F. Douglas Muschett. (Delray Beach, FL.: St. Lucie Press, 1997), pp. 131–149.

12. C. Lee Campbell and Walter W. Heck, *An Ecological Perspective on Sustainable Development.* In *Principles of Sustainable Development.* Edited by F. Douglas Muschett. (Delray Beach, FL.: St. Lucie Press, 1997), pp. 47–66.

13. See endnote 11 above.

14. See endnote 6 above.

15. Chris Maser, *Resolving Environmental Conflict: Towards Sustainable Community Development* (Delray Beach, FL.: St. Lucie Press, 1996).

16. Robert Chambers, *Rural Appraisal: Rapid, Relaxed and Participatory* (Sussex, UK: Institute of Development Studies, 1992) p. 90.

17. Roger Porkess, *The HarperCollins Dictionary of Statistics* (New York: HarperCollins Publishers, 1991).

18. See endnote 7 above.

19. For a discussion of some of these techniques see Jacob Cohen, *Statistical Analysis for Behavior Sciences* (New Jersey: Lawrence Erlbaum Associates, 1998). See also Bruce Tuckman, *Conducting Educational Research* (Chicago, IL.: Harcourt Brace Jovanovich Publishers, 1988).

20. Lorna Michael Butler, Colette Dephelps, and Robert E. Howell, *Focus Groups: A Tool for Understanding Community Perceptions and Experiences,* Western Regional Extensional Publication No. 0128. (Pullman, WA.: Washington State University, 1995), p. 1. See also Richard A. Krueger and Mary Anne Casey, *Focus Groups: A Practical Guide for Applied Research* (Thousand Oaks, CA.: Sage Publications, 2000).

21. Jeanne L. Kretschmer, *Women in Development: A Small Business Workshop.* In *Proceedings of the International Conference on Sustainable Village-Based Development.* (Fort Collins, CO.: Colorado State University, 1993), Sept. 27–Oct. 1.

22. See endnote 16 above.

23. Jim Rough, *Self-Evaluation: Ideas for Participatory Evaluation of Rural Community Development Projects* (Oklahoma City, OK.: World Neighbors, 1992), p. 17.

24. Jean Houston, *Creating a Sacred Psychology.* Wrekin Trust Cassette No. 81, Hereford England. In Howard Sasportas, *The Twelve Houses* (London, England: Thorsons, 1985), 400 pages.

25. Andrea Vierra and Judith Pollock, *Reading Educational Research* (Scottsdale, AZ.: Gorsuch Scarisbrick Publishers, 1988), 347 pages.

26. See endnote 25 above.

27. Michael Quinn Patton, *How to Use Qualitative Methods* (Newsbury Park, CA.: Sage Publications, 1987).

28. See endnote 27 above.

29. Daniel Yankelovich, *Coming to Public Judgment: Making Democracy Work in a Complex World* (Syracuse, NY.: Syracuse University Press, 1991), 290 pages.

30. Egon G. Guba and Yvonna S. Lincoln, *Effective Evaluation: Improving the Usefulness of Evaluation Results through Responsive and Naturalistic Approaches* (San Francisco, CA.: Jossey-Bass, 1981), 423 pages.

31. See endnote 25 above.

32. Edgar P. Yoder, *Validation and Verification of Qualitative Data Analysis,* Unpublished class note, Department of Agricultural and Extension Education. (University Park, PA.: Pennsylvania State University, 1993).

33. Thomas H. Wonnacott and Ronal J. Wonnacott, *Introductory Statistics* (New York: John Willey & Sons, Inc., 1969).

34. See endnote 33 above, p. 19.

35. See Basic handbooks on statistical data analysis such as David Moore and George McCabe's *Introduction to the Practice of Statistics* (New York: W.H. Freeman and Co., 1999) for detailed discussion of these inferential statistics and how to use them.

36. L. R. Gay, *Educational Research: Competencies for Analysis and Application* (Columbus, OH.: Merrill Publishing Co., 1987).

37. Paul Hawken, *The Ecology of Commerce* (New York: Harper-Collins Publishers, 1994), p. 4.

38. Sustainable Farmers Association, Strategic Plan 2000–2005 (draft), Sustainable Farmers Association of Northeast Minnesota, April, 2000.

39. Institute of Cultural Affairs, *Participant Workbook: Technology of Participation, Group Facilitation Methods* (AZ.: Institute of Cultural Affairs, 1994).

40. See endnote 37 above, p. xiii

41. See endnote 37 above, p. 35.

42. Jim Rugh, *Contributions of Participatory Evaluation to Sustainable Village-Based Development.* Proceedings of the International Conference on Sustainable Village-Based Development. (Fort Collins, CO.: Colorado State University, 1993), pp. 1815–1832.

43. Everett M. Rogers, *Diffusion of Innovations* 4th ed. (New York: The Free Press, 1995), p. xvi.

44. Our discussion of these elements of communication is partly based on Everett M. Rogers, *Diffusion of Innovations* (New York: The Free Press, 1995), 519 pages.

45. See endnote 44 above.

46. See endnote 44 above.

47. Niels G. Roling and M. Annemarie E. Wagemakers, *A New Practice: Facilitating Sustainable Agriculture.* In *Facilitating Sustainable Agriculture: Participatory Learning and Adaptive Management in Times of Environmental Uncertainty.* Edited by N. G. Roling and M. A. E. Wagemakers, (Cambridge, UK: Cambridge University Press, 1998), p. 8.

48. See endnote 44 above.

49. See endnote 44 above.

50. For a discussion of how to use specific methods or tools appropriately see Pat Calvert (ed.), *Communicator's Handbook: Tools, Techniques, and Technology* 4th ed. (Gainesville, FL.: Maupin House, 1999), 232 pages; Marie-Therese Feuerstein, *Partners in Evaluation* (London, England: Macmillian Publishers, 1986), Chapter 5, 196 pages; Lynn Lyons Morris, Carol Taylor Fitz-Gibbon, and Marie E. Freeman, *How to Communicate Evaluation Findings* (Newsbury Park, CA: Sage Publications, 1987), 92 pages.

51. Ulrich Nitsch, *The Art of Environmental Communication.* In *Knowledge and Action in the Environmental Field.* Edited by Lars J. Lundgren. (Swedish Environmental Protection Agency, In Press).

52. The following steps are based in part on "Communication Strategy Worksheet" by J. Cordell Hatch and "Strategy Worksheet" by H. A. Carey, unpublished class handouts, Department of Agriculture and Extension Education (University Park, PA.: Penn State University).

53. See endnote 42 above.

54. Lewis Carroll, *Alice's Adventures in Wonderland* (New York: Doubleday, Doran, & Co., 1933).

55. Stephen Arroyo, *Exploring Jupiter* (Sebastopol, CA.: CRCS Publications, 1996).

56. For a discussion of how lack of time, lack of skill, and lack of financial resources affect evaluation and possible solutions to these problems, see: Daniel Selener, Christopher Purdy, and Gabriela Zapata, *Documenting, Evaluating, and Learning from Our Development Projects* (Quito, Ecuador: International Institute of Reconstruction, 1998).

57. See endnote 42 above.

58. Our discussion of the Edwards Dam is based on Glenn Adams, "Fish Are Swimming Upstream after Maine Dam Removal," The

Associated Press, in *Democrat-Herald* (Albany, OR.) and *Gazette-Times* (Corvallis, OR.), Nov. 7, 1999.

59. Jennifer Greene, *One Definition of Participatory Evaluation,* Presented at the Joint Meeting of the Minnesota American Evaluation Association and the Minnesota Evaluation Studies Institute, St. Paul, Minnesota, May 17–19, 2000.

60. See endnote 59 above.

61. See endnote 15 above.

62. The discussions of values and aspects of vision follows Laurence G. Boldt, *Zen and the Art of Making a Living* (New York: Penguin/Arkana, 1993).

63. The Associated Press, "Ah-choo, Arizona No Longer Haven for Allergy Sufferers," *Corvallis Gazette-Times* (Corvallis, OR.), March 25, 1997.

64. William E. Ebomoyi, Okechukwu M. Ukaga, John B. Cooney, Jen Christiansen, Christopher Mecklin, and Amanda Febo, State of Colorado Abstinence Education Evaluation Research Study, 1999. Colorado Department of Public Health and Environment, Denver CO., 99 pages.

I

APPENDIX

EVALUATION OF MINNESOTA REGIONAL SUSTAINABLE DEVELOPMENT PARTNERSHIP PROJECTS: A CASE STUDY

Okechukwu Ukaga *

University of Minnesota

The "Regional Sustainable Development Partnerships" (RSDP) is a unique and fresh approach to fulfilling the University of Minnesota's land-grant mission of serving the people of Minnesota through education, research, and outreach. The RSDP works to sustain Minnesota communities by addressing locally identified, social-environmental issues that deal with agriculture, natural resources, and tourism, as well as alternative energy, and sustainable community development.

The Minnesota Legislator has provided funding for five Regional Partnerships located in the Northeast, Southeast, Central, Northwest, and West-Central parts of the state:

- The Northeast Regional Partnership, of which I am the director, covers all of St. Louis, Cook, and Carlton Counties, as well as parts of Koochiching, Itasca, Aitkin, and

* Okechukwu Ukaga is the Executive Director of Northeast Minnesota Sustainable Development Partnership, and working with the other RSDP staff and stakeholders, he provided leadership for the design and implementation of the RSDP project evaluation discussed in this paper.

Crow Wing counties. The bulk of this region is known ecologically as the Northern and Southern Superior Uplands.

- The Southeast Regional Partnership encompasses all or nearly all of Olmsted, Fillmore, Houston, Goodhue, Winona, and Wabasha Counties, as well as small portions of Mower and Dodge counties, an area that may generally be defined as Rochester Plateau and Blufflands.

- The Central Region covers all or parts of Cass, East Otter Tail, Becker, Hubbard, Crow Wing, Wadena, Todd, and Morrison Counties, an eco-region known as the Pine Moraine and Outwash plains.

- The Northwest Region covers Kittson, Roseau, Lake of the Woods, Marshal, Pennington, Red Lake, Polk, Norman, Mahnomen, Clay, and Wilkin Counties. The bulk of this region may be described ecologically as including the Aspen Parklands portions of the Laurentia Peatlands and the Red River Valley.

- The West-Central Region serves Big Stone, Chippewa, Douglas, Grant, Kandiyohi, Lac qui Parle, Pope, Renville, Stevens, Swift, Traverse, and Yellow Medicine Counties. It borders the Dakotas, is part of the Minnesota Red River Basin, and includes parts of the Red River Prairie and Hardwood Hills.

- Additional Partnerships are expected to cover the remaining areas in the future.

Each of these Regional Partnerships has an Executive Director and a 15- to 20-member Board of Directors composed primarily of local citizens, as well as a few research and extension faculty from the University of Minnesota. Board members are usually selected by an RSDP Task Force or Coordinating Committee that identifies the initial regional team of about five people, representing diverse interests and backgrounds in the area, who then recruit additional members and activate the regional program in accordance with guidelines provided by the task force.

The specific steps in choosing a board member include: (1) a formal, written nomination of the candidate; (2) the candidate completes a written application that allows the candidate to provide his or her name, address, and response to two questions: What qualifies me to serve on the regional board. Why do I want to participate in this process?; (3) team members screen applications, select new board members, and establish rotations. In the Northeast, for example, the term of office for board members is three years and is renewable once. This policy helps the board to find new members and encourage new ideas. At the same time, the board maintains some current members through a staggered rotation process that replaces only a third of the members every year.

The citizen-faculty board envisions a sustainable future for its region and supports projects to achieve the vision. The role of the Board is to share program principles; invite and engage participation of citizens and the University; manage the process; make rules; serve as investors, conveners, and referees; and leverage money for Partnership projects. The Board of Directors looks for potential projects; makes decisions about new projects; reviews existing projects; attends "listening" meetings; and evaluates the results of completed projects.

The three foundational principles guiding the work of the RSDPs were established by the RSDP Steering Committee based on the Principles of Sustainable Development for Minnesota that were adopted on September 18, 1996, by the Minnesota Round Table on Sustainable Development. These principles form the basis on which each partnership selects and evaluates its respective projects. They are:

- Sustainable Development—addressing issues according to the principles of sustainable development, which means investing in research, education, and outreach that advance the understanding and achievement of local and regional sustainability.

- Active Citizenship—local citizen participation, including shared leadership in designing and implementing projects in their region.

- University Involvement—building effective relationships among citizens, their communities, and the University of Minnesota.

Project evaluation is important to the Regional Partnerships for three reasons. First, to assure excellence in programming by applying what has been learned from the evaluations to continuously improve our work. Second, to generate good data through evaluation that we can use to effectively inform our stakeholders and the general public about our program and its accomplishments.

Participation is important not only because it is one of the RSDP bedrock principles but also because we believe that, if an evaluation is done with the full participation of those who are affected by the project, the results are likely to be more realistic and valuable. Further, because the people constitute a major segment of the decision-making body concerning the RSDP program and projects, they need to understand the evaluation results and can best do so through involvement in the whole process.

With the foregoing in mind, the question is: Can participatory evaluation help a group assess their projects in accordance with the principles of sustainable development? The observations presented here provide some insights into this question.

What Is to Be Evaluated

Because we are interested in evaluating the performance of the individual projects we fund, as well as how well we are doing with regard to the RSDP principles, each evaluation is designed to assess how well it is: (a) achieving the stated objectives and (b) abiding by the three aforementioned, bedrock principles of sustainability.

With the purpose of evaluation clear, the RSDP staff and statewide coordinating committee determined through an iterative process that, to meet their evaluation objectives, they needed to find answers to specific questions about: (1) Project Description, (2) Sustainable Development, (3) University Involvement, (4) Active Citizenship, (5) Lessons Learned, and (6) Funding.

Project Description
- Goals: What is the project designed to accomplish?
- Approach: What are the steps or actions taken to achieve these goals?
- Outcomes: What tangible results did you achieve?

Sustainable Development
- How did this project enhance environmental, social, and economic sustainability?
- What difference did the project make in the community or among participants to enhance sustainability in each of these areas: environment, community, and economics?

University Involvement
- How did the project enhance the relationship among the local communities, the University of Minnesota, and other partners?

Active Citizenship
- How were local citizens and communities actively involved in the planning, implementation, and evaluation of this project?
- How did the project enhance the capacity for active citizenship among participants in the community?

Lessons Learned
- What lessons did we learn from this project?
- What, if anything, would we do differently next time?

Funding

- How much funding for this project was provided by the RSDP?

- How much funding for this project was received from others sources?

- In what ways (other than funding) was the Regional Partnership helpful in assuring the success of this project or future projects?

- In what ways (other than funding) could the Regional Partnership be helpful in assuring the success of future projects?

We decided to focus on these six things because we determined that such data were sufficient for answering our evaluation questions. Specifically, the project description would tell us what goals a given project was designed to achieve, the steps or actions taken to achieve these goals, and what outcomes or tangible results would be achieved by the project. With such data, we would be able to answer one of our two main evaluation questions: whether or not a given project has achieved (or is achieving) the stated objectives.

Answers to questions about sustainable development, active citizenship, and university involvement, would tell us if and how the project: (a) enhanced social, environmental, and economic sustainability in the area; (b) strengthened the relationship among the University of Minnesota, local citizens, communities, and other partners; and (c) engaged local communities and enhanced the capacity for active citizenship among participants and within the community. Again, with the above data, we can answer the other major evaluation question we have: namely, how well are the projects abiding by the three RSDP bedrock principles of sustainability.

The questions about lessons learned allows us to get feedback from the project leaders and participants about their experiences and insights regarding all aspects of the projects, including what worked well, what did not work so well, and we could do differently to improve this project or future projects. Respondents are given the further option of making additional comments in an open-ended format. Together, these data provide useful insights not only about the achievements and challenges of the specific project but also about the RSDP effort in general and how it is received by various stakeholders. Finally, the questions about funding and other sources/types of support tells us the total resources that were invested in a given project and how much of that was leveraged from various sources. This knowledge allows us and other stakeholders to judge the project's benefits, achievements, and outcomes within the context of resources invested. It also gives a good sense of who is supporting the project and by how much.

Evaluation Methods and Criteria

To assure consistency, efficiency, and effectiveness data were collected primarily by means of a questionnaire developed by the RSDP group. Like the entire system of evaluation, the instrument was designed in a participatory and iterative fashion. One of the regional executive directors produced an initial draft of the evaluation form based on the group's objectives and the questions they were interested in finding answers to. The draft was then reviewed by each participant, as well as discussed by the whole group, and was revised accordingly. This review and revision process was repeated a few times until the group produced an instrument that was unanimously accepted for use in collecting data about partnership projects.

Using the questionnaire, RSDP staff members elicited answers to the questions noted above, as well as demographic information: project title, starting and ending dates, names and contact information of community and university partners, regions of the state involved in the project, the type of project (for example, agriculture, natural resources, tourism, food security, energy, and so on), and who submitted the report on what date.

Project leaders are typically asked to complete the evaluation form at the end of each project in order for us to: (1) document project activities and results, (2) determine whether the project succeeded in accomplishing its stated objects, and (3) assess how useful and effective it was in applying and advancing the RSDP principles of sustainability. Additional methods, such as verbal interviews, progress reports, and presentations are also used to collect and disseminate data in order for us to augment the data collected and shared via questionnaires. Although we use a variety of methods to collect data, there is scant variation in the evaluation criteria we employ, particularly with respect to: project description, RSDP bedrock principles, lessons learned, and funding because we wanted to assure consistency across projects and regions in other to make sure we are collecting the same data. This is critical since we need to be able to aggregate the data in order to compare results among various projects, across regions, and over time. We cannot do any of these if we use different evaluation criteria. Yet, while people work together to design and conduct an evaluation, we find that some differences in perception and nuance can still be detected among the people involved. Here is a sample of the differences we find:

1. "What we are evaluating is the success of citizens using their university for community-defined sustainability opportunities in agriculture and natural resources. Evaluation criteria include level of activity, outcomes for specific projects, changes or improvement within the university system to respond to community request or opportunities."

2. "We are evaluating the projects we fund: their connection to local citizens and the university, the amount [of resources] we provided, who we are going to work with, the outcome for the project, how many years those projects have been funded, and if all criteria have been met. Evaluation criteria

are: (1) make sure that we meet the funding requirement and (2) that we are credible with our outcomes regarding the three criteria in our brochure, that is, projects initiated and supported by local citizens; partnering local citizens with University of Minnesota staff and resources; and addressing regional issues in agriculture and natural resources, economics, human development, education and long-term sustainability."

3. "The [evaluation] form tells us a bit about how we define the project quality and partners. On the qualitative side, we are evaluating how well we are doing with our bedrock principles. Here we may have more variance due to who is writing the report than variance on actual project. It depends entirely on the person writing the evaluation report and his writing ability. With regard to criteria, the good thing is that we are asking the same questions about how we meet our principles: the questions about citizen participation, sustainability, and university involvement. But it would be better if we can come up with a matrix that we can quantify. For instance, there is a difference between simply counting the number of people involved in a project and capturing the depth or level of participation."

4. "The purpose of the evaluation is to know the people we are working with, their evaluation of what they have learned, and how they have met the goals (or not) relative to our bedrock principles. Each project has a set of goals and we look at how well they met these goals, the level of where the goals have been met (or not met), and our principles."

5. "We are qualitatively evaluating project outcomes based upon the goals defined at the outset of a project. This is what seems consistent across all regions and projects. The evaluation method seems to be a self-evaluation by project sponsors in consultation with board members and other interested parties. The evaluation criteria include our three

bedrock principles and sustainability criteria, as well as the project goals as identified by the project sponsor in concert with the regional board. Data collection is typically through written reports and interviews with project sponsors, partners, and other affected parties."

6. "It is very important that we continue to use a standard evaluation form and system across all regions and projects to collect a minimum set of required information even though different regions and projects may need to collect additional data over and above the minimum."

Data Analysis and Interpretation

Statewide, our analysis and interpretation of data has been typically inductive and entails the gathering and aggregating a lot of information because we are primarily interested in combining all the data and distilling its essential characteristics, patterns, and summaries. To this end, we generally use brief qualitative summaries, descriptive statistics analysis, and communication of findings. We use brief summaries partly because our target audiences tend to want such brief, uncomplicated reports; and partly because we, quite frankly, have not deemed it a high priority to spend more time and resources doing extensive data analysis and reporting. We spend most of our time and resources planning and implementing projects. Recently, however, we spent a little more time and produced a voluminous evaluation matrix with a lot of data about our projects. The reception was mixed. While some felt it was useful to have all that information in one document, others suggested that it was too big and to complex to be useful; that very few people who need to know about our work will actually take time to read such a large report. Overall, the method of analysis has been largely qualitative at the minimum.

On an individual project basis, however, the use of quantitative data, especially inferential statistics (for example, soil drainage

increases by x percent based on methods y and z), has been spo-
radic because we have not stressed the collection of such data due
to a lack of consensus and/or strong interest among all the stakeholders. While we have used these data to learn what we need to
know project-by-project, we have not done as good a job with our
evaluations to see how we are doing on an overall program basis.
Reflecting on how we analyze RSDP project data, one regional
director noted that we typically "count-up numbers and synthesize
data" but we are "not big on synthesis. When I summarize the
data," she continued, what "I see is that we have a good distribution of projects across our areas of interest, and that we have
engaged a broad spectrum of stakeholders, which means that we
are expanding our reach. But I suspect there is more information
that can be gleaned from the data if we are more systematic in our
analysis."

Our conclusions are sometimes based, as one director
observed, "on what may be subjective but nonetheless valid
interpretation of aggregated data." As another noted, we "keep
pretty much contact with the project. So that adds to what is
written. We know more than is written."

We use evaluation data in a variety of ways with board members and citizens in meetings, discussions, and so on. We also
used these data to justify how money is spent on projects, to
measure success, and to explore fundamental questions concerning such things as how we approach the bigger picture of sustainability. In addition, Board members meet with project teams
as necessary to examine and discuss the team's plan, progress,
and results. In the Central Region, for example, each team of a
funded project attends the annual meeting with a progress report
in hand and presents it to the Board. The report, as well as any
additional information concerning a given project, is then analyzed to make sure the progress and outcomes are satisfactory.
For those projects requiring more than one-year of support, the
Board usually makes previous year, satisfactory progress a condition for further support.

Communicating Findings

We use a variety of methods and media in order to share the results of our project evaluation. The methods include: verbal presentations, meetings, networking with others interested in the project, written reports, letters, e-mails, and web sites. These methods are chosen on a case by case, project by project, audience by audience basis and are based on their feasibility, effectiveness, and required resources (financial, human, technical, and so on). The media include: radio, television, newspapers, magazines, seasonal tabloids, and various other publications. The media used is selected, among other things, on: (1) which media would be most effective in delivering the messages to the intended audience(s) and (2) which ones would be relatively easy, efficient, affordable, and accessible for all persons involved.

We use an on-line searchable database to enhance sharing the results of reports on project evaluations. We also tailor reports, presentations, and other forms of communication to fit specific audiences, such as legislators, University administrators, and community members. One partnership used a video that tells their story in order to introduce themselves to the people of their region and share what had been accomplished. This approach has been credited with the dramatic move of that regional program from near obscurity several months ago to good public awareness today. The following is a sample of opinions from people involved in use and communication of results from the evaluation of a RSDP:

1. "Project reports, board meetings, the evaluation database, and our web site are some of the methods/media we have used to communicate. In our recent evaluation summary, some descriptive information from the evaluation database was gleaned for the project matrix."

2. "We use the data in our yearly newsletters. We highlight projects results. We use the evaluation reports as part of our

annual meeting. My board sees all the reports. Presentations add to the reports. I think our communication is more internal than external, except for the recent report prepared for our authorizers, which I see as a promotional piece. This helped us pull the numbers together to show our internal and external audiences how we are doing. It is what folks want now. But I would hope we take the deeper approach (for example, five year plan; ask how are we doing with the bigger picture of sustainability?)."

3. "We used the information to answer to my board about what has happened to this project. It helps to put something on paper. Communication is easier and more effective when results are concrete and documented. The evaluation provided very good documentation of impacts, of what happened ("so what") and how the goals are met."

4. "The evaluation database has worked well as a repository of descriptive information."

5. " I think we should only target two groups: (1) opinion leaders within the University like the President, Board of Regents, key administrators, and faculty and (2) key community leaders that carry our message. I think we should have a list of these two groups and go after them. We are doing way too much. I am not a big fan of new logo, video, web site and so on. We are targeting everyone right now and I do not think it has worked very well so far."

Lessons Learned

While the process we used to develop and implement this evaluation system was participatory and iterative, it took considerable time, patience, collaborative effort, and a skilled team leader to make it happen. Everyone involved liked the process and agreed that it has been healthy. Participants also told us where and how the evaluation system could be improved. One observed that it has been "very iterative so far with a lot of back and forth. But it is not aimed precisely enough. We have tried to satisfy too many objectives." Another said, "I like the process of how we developed our evaluation. What it has done for us is make us credible. We use the "matrix" from year to year. But our reports need to be short to enhance readership." And yet a third participant noted that, "it has not worked so well to date in consistently providing information that is important to understanding the performance of a project and its impacts, both quantitative (such as number of community, faculty, student participants; amount of funds leveraged by type; and other quantitative impacts) and broader qualitative information, such as what behavior might have been changed as a result of this project."

Further, we found that no matter how participatory an evaluation is, one cannot assume that people are always paying attention to the available options or the decisions being made. This lack of attention can lead to complaints, inconsistency, and/or reduction in level of compliance. For instance, there isn't a shared understanding among the people of all regions about when to prepare an evaluation or what to include. Some people begin preparing an evaluation report when their project begins while others do so towards their project's conclusion.

Too much latitude can lead to inconsistency that affects the number of projects represented in the database and how fully they are discussed. It is also a little confusing for the reader and does not always present a clear idea of a project's aims and outcomes. We therefore learned that some "top down" directives, shared agreements, and strong leadership is helpful to ensure all participants pull together in one direction and interpret instructions, methods, data, and analysis in the same way. Otherwise, people tend to be fragmented in their approaches to the various aspects of evaluation. I find we need stronger directives to ensue the unity of our approach to evaluation. One of the executive directors commented, "There is almost too much latitude for my liking."

Not being able to easily enter data on the web site was another challenge we did not anticipate. The problems had to do with bugs and related technical difficulties associated with the initial versions of the on-line database designed for the evaluation. This vexing circumstance was a simple, even if painful, reminder that unanticipated problems do come up; and high-tech solutions can come with their own technical challenges. Hence it is advisable to think carefully about the need for and appropriateness of any technology relative to evaluation objectives, target audience, available resources (technical, human, financial, time), and so on before including it as part of your evaluation system.

Another development to which we had to adapt was our realization, while preparing reports for some of our authorizers, that we needed information on such numbers as: community members, faculty participants, student participants, total project cost, and type/proportion of other sources of funds that we did not have in the database from data collected already. Some of these were reported infrequently and sometimes inconsistently, while others were not reported at all. It was important that we fill the gaps, especially since our Deans (and to a lesser degree some other stakeholders) had expressed the interest in this type of information. So we went back and collected these data for all previous and current projects and agreed to do so routinely in the future. As a result, we made some structural and process changes to our evaluation system. Notably, we decided to modify our instrument to collect these additional data, and to add a couple of fill-in-the-blanks to our on-line database to accommodate the additional data.

The complexity and depth of what we are trying to do is another issue. The more we worked to perfect the evaluation, the more we came to appreciate its complexity and how hard it is to capture completely by using the same format to report the various kinds of projects. We learned, therefore, that it is critical to use multiple tools and approaches, including both quantitative and qualitative methods, in order to capture the complexity. One person suggested that we need to develop and use an index in order to more easily and realistically compare data across projects and settings. Although such an index would helps us know if and how we are making a difference in the community or within a project, it would mean a shift in our evaluation objectives and methods.

As one regional director observed, "there seems to be some resistance to changing things. I understand not having to change things. But we should be happy to change it if we can make it better because we hardly knew what we needed to know at the beginning." We clearly need to be flexible in our approach to evaluations by periodically reflecting on its effectiveness and ways to improve it.

Summary and Conclusion

This case study illustrates how participatory evaluation can be used by a group interested in fostering sustainable development to determine: what is to be evaluated; the evaluation criteria; the methods and instruments for generating necessary data; and how to analyze, interpret, and communicate findings. In brief, we have learned that a good evaluation of any project has some important steps including: (1) articulating the groups' principles of sustainable development; (2) crafting a vision, goals, and objectives—to determine what is wanted, why, and what its components might be; (3) deciding what to evaluate and choosing indicators to measure or monitor that; (4) determining and using appropriate sources, timing, instruments, and method to collect data; (5) analyzing data to determine if what is being done is really what was intended, what improvements (if any) need to be made, and if the project has achieved what the people wanted it to; and (6) using and communicating findings.

We have also learned that the knowledge gleaned from these steps is cumulative and sets up a self-reinforcing feedback loop that is directly dependent on the quality of the data collected in the sequential steps. If a step is inadequately conducted, interpretation of the entire data is compromised. It is critical, therefore, that each step is given the attention to detail required to ensure, as much as humanly possible, that the design, collection, analysis, interpretation, integration, and communication of data are complete and of the highest integrity in order to best serve the stakeholders.

2

APPENDIX

Organization of the data generated in the June 25, 1999, meeting of the Northeast Region Sustainable Development Partnership (Minnesota), the board members' insiders' framework (vision, desired outcomes, and ideas for action).

Vision

1. People would be supportive, or at least neutral, to the concept of sustainability; many would know how and want to live sustainably.

2. Communities in northeast Minnesota would be vibrant and healthy and would maintain their character and local culture.

3. People would work to protect healthy, abundant, and regenerating natural resources.

4. People would waste less, consume less, and recycle more.

5. People would build trust, question assumptions, and be committed to innovation.

6. Efficient methods of transportation would be available.

7. The resource base would be sustained or improved from an ecosystem point of view. People would respect its value.

8. There would be more value-added local industry based on local renewable resources, with more goods and services produced locally.

9. High quality education would be provided.

10. There would be an interdependence based on a balanced exchange of necessary goods and ideas while minimizing nonsustainable transportation.

11. Enough quality jobs would be produced so people could live with dignity; little poverty.

12. Healthy people empower themselves through involvement in planning and decision making in order to maintain a healthy community and society.

13. People would live and work in such a way that there would be less stress on individuals, communities, and the environment.

14. Citizens would respect the University of Minnesota's partnership as evidenced by requesting relevant information to make decisions.

15. Communities would depend on more small enterprises rather than a few big businesses.

16. Economic growth would be planned in order to create and maintain a desired future condition.

17. Decisions concerning land use and development would be made in a way that promotes sustainability and efficient use of infrastructure.

18. Long-term population trends and how they affect sustainability would be monitored.

Desired Outcomes

1. Public awareness:
   - education
   - more grant money to northeastern Minnesota
   - private investment to add jobs
   - gain valuable information and/or data

- higher paid employment opportunities
- enjoying, using, and appreciating natural resources

2. Raise public awareness of locally grown quality food:
   - bigger farmer's market.
   - sales throughout the nongrowing season
   - buy local products in supermarkets
   - producers cooperative-network liaison with sellers
   - Sustainable Farming Association helps get Duluth to support farmer's market in Duluth

3. Sustainable housing to meet the needs; development, and marketing of such.

4. Okey will have a sustainable car.

5. Each community has a plan to deal with sewer, water, industry, and historical precedence.

6. Education on property tax structure: develop a property tax structure that promotes sustainability.

7. Appropriate and sustainable set-backs from lake shore, for example, a vegetative buffer zone.

8. Consider future economy of precious metals.

9. Stakeholders are actively engaged.

10. Public policy will favor sustainability in a sustainable form.

11. People will understand and support sustainability.

12. People understand how their actions affect systems and other people around them and will promote a systems approach to planning.

13. Respect and appreciation for private investment:
    - increase in tax base for local governments
    - adequate data showing results of capital investment

14. Enhanced awareness of sustainability by developing a web site for Northeast Region Sustainable Development Partnership linked to other sustainability sites, communities, and the university.

15. More cooperation:

- wider variety of ways to work with other organizations
- agencies offer remediation
- more trustworthy organizations, more trusting relationships
- better communication and more trust.

Ideas for Action

1. Conduct research on the property tax structure.

2. Conduct research on the impact of investment on tax base and infrastructure, quality of life, and external realities.

3. Conduct research on how the legislature exerts pressure on local units of government—"unfounded mandates," and how their policies affect local decisions.

4. Produce newsletters to inform public.

5. Inform small communities through local newspaper articles.

6. Conduct public relations through public radio and television.

7. Make presentations in schools, that is, through School Nature Area Program.

8. Make presentations to government officials.

9. Involve people as we move ahead.

10. Produce examples of sustainable development.

11. Participate in Town Meetings and/or sponsored speakers.

12. Create a web site.

13. Hold panel discussions.

14. Research different ways to educate northeastern Minnesota about the issue of sustainability.

15. Educate citizens about the results of research projects.

16. Add farmers and consumers to farmer's market.

17. Encourage efforts to create value-added products.

18. Look at direct marketing of agricultural produce.

19. Get the University of Minnesota to network their marketing plan.

20. Establish a food literacy campaign.

21. Address regional meat processing with respect to the need for more processing plants in the area.

22. Look at true cost accountability of local foods vs. those shipped in.

23. Encourage people to garden and share and/or trade excess produce.

24. Encourage on-farm research to evaluate and disseminate processes that foster sustainable agricultural.

25. Develop a network liaison between producers and buyers of agricultural produce in northeastern Minnesota.

26. Teach people to process their own food.

27. Applied economic evaluation to housing patterns and/or taxation.

28. Join with other organizations to conduct research on sustainable methods of transportation.

29. Educate the community prior to forming a community task force on planning and development—involve citizens (broad based).

30. Gather data on planning.

31. Choose to use Arrowhead Regional Development Corporation.

32. Put money into planning.

33. Involve people from the community in our subcommittees.

34. Listen to people's needs.

35. Ask people to work with the University of Minnesota Sustainable Development Partnership in order to plan and promote sustainable development in the area.

36. Conduct research and education on public policy.

37. Develop and utilize central planning maps for communities to promote sustainable development.

38. Board members will write articles for local papers.

39. Survey interactions between government and individuals around issues of sustainability; offer our help where useful; encourage communication and involvement by all citizen interested in sustainable development.

40. Create forums in which groups of like mind can come together.

41. Educate decision makers about results of research conducted on land-use trends and their effects.

42. Conduct research on appropriate ways to provide an economic base while living sustainably (for example, work toward increased set-backs on Lake Superior).

3

APPENDIX

Reorganization of the data generated in the June 25, 1999, meeting of the Northeast Region Sustainable Development Partnership (Minnesota), using the Jan and Cornelia Flora's outsiders' framework.

Outcomes Identified by Institutional Actors

1. High use of local skills and abilities (human capital)
   a. People will know how to and want to live sustainably
   b. High quality education provided
2. Many networks and good communication (social capital)
   a. People empowered by involvement in planning and decision making
   b. More cooperation, better communication, and more trusting relationships
3. Innovation, responsibility, and adaptability (social capital)
   a. Less stress on individuals, communities, and the environment
   b. Greater emphasis on diversity, less on bigness
   c. Question assumptions; commit to innovations
4. Healthy ecosystems with multiple community benefits (natural capital)

    a. Healthy, abundant, regenerating natural resources

    b. Enjoying, using, and appreciating natural resources

5. Appropriately diverse and healthy economy (financial capital)

    a. Vibrant, healthy communities that maintain their character and culture

    b. Enough quality jobs for people to live in dignity; little poverty

    c. Interdependence: balanced exchange of goods with minimum nonsustainable transportation

    d. Planned economic growth relative to desired conditions

Natural Capital

Activities

- Join with other organizations in research on sustainable transportation

Outputs

- Less waste and consumption
- Land use and development decisions promote sustainability and efficient use of infrastructure

Outcomes

1. Use of local skills and abilities

    a. People will know how to and want to live sustainably

    b. High quality education provided

    c. People empowered by their involvement in planning and decision making

    d. Cooperation, better communication, and more trusting relationships

3. Innovation, responsibility, adaptability

   a. Less human, communication, and environmental stressors

   b. Diversity, not bigness

   c. Question assumptions; commit to innovations

4. Healthy ecosystems with multiple community benefits

   a. Regenerating natural resources

   b. Enjoying, using, and appreciating natural resources

5. Diverse and healthy economy

   a. Vibrant, healthy communities that maintain their character and culture

   b. Enough quality jobs for people to live in dignity; little poverty

   c. Balanced exchange of goods with minimum nonsustainable transportation

   d. Planned appropriate economic growth

Social Capital

Activities

- Develop network liaison between producers and buyers (direct marketing)
- Get the university to do network marketing plan
- Educate community prior to forming a community task force on planning broad-based citizen involvement
- Involve community people in subcommittees
- Encourage people to garden and share and/or trade
- Ask people to get involved
- Expand farmer's market
- Buy local products in supermarket
- Producer co-op that networks with sellers

Outputs

- Partnership between the university and citizens
- People understand how their actions affect systems and others
- Wider variety of ways to work with other organizations

Outcomes

1. Use of local skills and abilities
   a. People will know how and want to live sustainably
   b. High quality education provided
2. Networks and good communication
   a. People empowered by involvement in planning and decision making
   b. Cooperation, better communication, and more trusting relationships
3. Innovation, responsibility, adaptability
   a. Less human, communication, and environmental stressors
   b. Diversity, not bigness
   c. Question assumptions; commit to innovations
4. Healthy ecosystems with multiple community benefits
   a. Regenerating natural resources
   b. Enjoying, using, and appreciating natural resources
5. Diverse and healthy economy
   a. Vibrant, healthy communities that maintain their character and culture
   b. Enough quality jobs for people to live in dignity; little poverty
   c. Balanced exchange of goods with minimum nonsustainable transportation
   d. Planned appropriate economic growth

Human Capital

Activities

- Educate decision makers on research results regarding land use trends and their effects
- Produce examples for Atlas book (examples come from Northeast Region Sustainable Development Partnership activities to be disseminated as part of education, public relations, and accountability)
- Conduct research on how the legislature exerts pressure on local units of government—"unfounded mandates," and how their policies affect local decisions
- Contribute articles to small community newspapers
- Listen to peoples needs
- Set up food literacy campaign
- Monitor long-term population trends and how they effect sustainability in northeast Minnesota
- Establish web site for Northeast Region Sustainable Development Partnership linked to other sustainability sites, communities, and universities

Outputs

- Raise public awareness of locally grown quality food

Outcomes

1. Use of local skills and abilities
   a. People will know how to and want to live sustainably
   b. High quality education provided
2. Networks and good communication
   a. People empowered by their involvement in planning and decision making
   b. Cooperation, better communication, and more trusting relationships

3. Innovation, responsibility, adaptability
   a. Less human, community, and environmental stressors
   b. Diversity, not bigness
   c. Question assumptions; commit to innovations
4. Healthy ecosystems with multiple community benefits
   a. Regenerating natural resources
   b. Enjoying, using, and appreciating natural resources
5. Diverse and healthy economy
   a. Vibrant, healthy communities that maintain their character and culture
   b. Enough quality jobs for people to live in dignity; little poverty
   c. Balanced exchange of goods with minimum nonsustainable transportation
   d. Planned appropriate economic growth

Financial and/or Built Capital

Activities
- Conduct research on the impact of investment on tax base, infrastructure, quality of life, and external realities
- Put money into planning
- Applied economic evaluation of housing patterns and/or taxation
- Get more grant money

Outputs
- More value added to local industry based on renewable resources
- More efficient transportation
- Added jobs through private investment

- Sustainably built housing to meet needs
- Increased local government tax base
- Appreciation of private investment

Outcomes

1. Use of local skills and abilities
   a. People will know how to and want to live sustainably
   b. High quality education provided
2. Networks and good communication
   a. People empowered by their involvement in planning and decision making
   b. Cooperation, better communication and more trusting relationships
6. Innovation, responsibility, adaptability
   a. Less human, community, and environmental stressors
   b. Diversity, not bigness
   c. Question assumptions; commit to innovations
7. Healthy ecosystems with multiple community benefits
   a. Regenerating natural resources
   b. Enjoying, using, and appreciating natural resources
8. Diverse and healthy economy
   a. Vibrant, healthy communities that maintain their character and culture
   b. Enough quality jobs for people to live in dignity; little poverty
   c. Balanced exchange of goods with minimum nonsustainable transportation
   d. Planned appropriate economic growth

About the Authors

OKECHUKWU UKAGA is the Executive Director of Northeast Minnesota Sustainable Development Partnership, University of Minnesota. He is also an extension educator and associate professor of sustainable development with University of Minnesota Extension Service. Before coming to Minnesota, Dr. Ukaga served as Managing Director of the International Institute for Sustainable Development at Colorado State University for five years. In that capacity, he managed a variety of sustainable community development projects and worked with organizations and people from countries in Africa, South America, Asia, and the Middle East on such projects.

He was born in Nigeria and received a Ph.D. in agricultural and extension education, from Penn State University, an M.S. in education and an M.B.A. from Florida A & M University, and a Post Graduate Diploma in agricultural economics from the University of Nigeria. He has previously worked at Penn State University and Florida A & M University. He has traveled to India, Indonesia, and Nigeria to lecture on sustainable development. He is currently a member of the Minnesota Sea Grant College Board, and the Executive Board of Minnesota Evaluation Association. He is also a member of a Kettering Foundation funded national (USA) taskforce on the practice of public scholarship in land-grant institutions, and a member of a European Union funded international taskforce on evaluation of sustainable development. His current professional and research interests are in participatory planning and evaluation of sustainable development, alternative and distributed energy, sustainable management of private woodlands, assisting communities to achieve sustainable tourism and recreation, community food systems and agricultural development.

Okechukwu Ukaga has written and/or coauthored more than 50 publications. His latest books are *Renewing the Countryside—Minnesota* (2001, co-edited with Jan Joannides, Sara Bergan, Mark Ritchie, and Beth Waterhouse) and the forthcoming book *Sustainable Development in Africa* (2004, Africa World Press, co-edited with Osita Afoaku).

CHRIS MASER spent over 25 years as a research scientist in natural history and ecology in forest, shrub steppe, subarctic, desert, coastal, and agricultural settings. Trained primarily as a vertebrate zoologist, he was a research mammalogist in Nubia, Egypt, (1963–1964) with the Yale University Peabody Museum Prehistoric Expedition and was a research mammalogist in Nepal (1966–1967) for the U.S. Naval Medical Research Unit #3 based in Cairo, Egypt, where he participated in a study of tick-borne diseases. He conducted a three-year (1970–1973) ecological survey of the Oregon Coast for the University of Puget Sound, Tacoma, Washington. He was a research ecologist with the U.S. Department of the Interior, Bureau of Land Management for twelve years (1975–1987)—the last eight studying old-growth forests in western Oregon—and a landscape ecologist with the Environmental Protection Agency for one year (1990–1991).

Today Chris Maser is an independent author as well as an international lecturer, facilitator in resolving environmental conflicts, vision statements, and sustainable community development. He is also an international consultant in forest ecology and sustainable forestry practices.

Chris Maser has written over 260 publications, including the following books: *The Redesigned Forest* (1988); *Forest Primeval: The Natural History of an Ancient Forest* (1989); *Global Imperative: Harmonizing Culture and Nature* (1992); Sustainable Forestry: Philosophy, Science, and Economics (1994); *From the Forest to the Sea: The Ecology of Wood in Streams, Rivers, Estuaries, and Oceans* (1994, with James R. Sedell); *Resolving Environmental Conflict: Toward Sustainable Community Development* (1996); *Sustainable Community Development: Principles and Concepts* (1997); *Setting the Stage for Sustainability: A Citizen's Handbook* (1998, with Russ Beaton and Kevin Smith); *Vision and Leadership in Sustainable Development* (1998); *Mammals of the Pacific Northwest: From the Coast to the High Cascades* (1998); *Ecological Diversity in Sustainable Development: The Vital and Forgotten Dimension* (1999); *Reuniting Economy and Ecology in Sustainable Development (1999, with Russ Beaton); Planning for Sustainable Development* (2000, with Jane Silberstein); *Forest Certification in Sustainable Development: Healing the Landscape* (2000, with Walter Smith); and *The World Is in My Garden: A Journey of Consciousness* (2003, with Zane Maser), and *The Perpetual Consequences of Fear and Violence: Rethinking the Future* (2004).

He has worked and/or lectured in Canada, Egypt, France, Germany, Japan, Malaysia, Nepal, Slovakia, Switzerland, and various settings in the United States.